BERLITZ®

GERMAN
FOR TRAVELLERS

By the staff of Editions Berlitz

Library of Congress Catalog Card Number: 74-1976

First revised edition
14th printing 1982

Printed in Hungary

Editions Berlitz
1, avenue des Jordils
1000 Lausanne 6, Switzerland

Preface

In preparing this complete revision of *German for Travellers,*
we took into consideration a wealth of suggestions and criticisms received by phrase-book users around the world. As a
result, this new edition features:

a) a complete phonetic transcription throughout indicating
the pronunciation of all words and phrases you'll need to
know on your trip

b) special sections showing the replies your listener might
give to you. Just hand him the book and let him point to
the appropriate phrase. This is especially practical in
certain difficult situations (doctor, garage mechanic, etc.).

c) a complete revision of the section on Eating Out to make
it even more useful in a restaurant. Austrian and German
Swiss items have been included, too.

d) a tipping chart and a more comprehensive reference
section in the back of the book.

These are new features. They complement what has become
the world's most popular phrase-book series, helping you
with:

* all the phrases and supplementary vocabulary you'll need
on your trip

* a wide variety of tourist and travel facts, tips and useful
information

* quick reference through colour coding. The major features
of the contents are on the back cover. A complete index is
found inside.

These are just a few of the practical advantages. In addition, the book will prove a valuable introduction to life in Germany, Austria and Switzerland.

There's a comprehensive section on Eating Out, giving translations and explanations for practically anything one would find on a German menu; there's a complete Shopping Guide that will enable you to obtain virtually anything you want.

Trouble with the car? Turn to the mechanic's manual with its dual-language terms. Feeling ill? Our medical section provides the most rapid communication possible between you and the doctor.

To make the most of *German for Travellers,* we suggest that you start with the "Guide to Pronunciation". Then go on to "Some Basic Expressions". This not only gives you a minimum vocabulary; it helps you to pronounce the language.

We're particularly grateful to Mrs. C.A. Carl-Sime and Miss Sylvia Reul for their help in the preparation of this book and to Dr. T.J.A. Bennett who devised the phonetic transcription. We also wish to thank the German Central Tourist Association for its assistance.

We shall be very pleased to receive any comments, criticisms and suggestions that you think may help us in preparing future editions.

Thank you. Have a good trip.

Throughout this book, the symbols illustrated here indicate small sections where phrases have been compiled that your foreign listener might like to say to *you.* If you don't understand him, give him the book and let him point to the phrase in his language. The English translation is just beside it.

Basic Grammar

Here is the briefest possible outline of some essential features of German grammar.

Articles

All nouns in German are either masculine, feminine or neuter, and they are classified by the article which precedes them.

1. Definite article (the):

Plural:

masc. *der* **Mann**	the man	*die* **Männer**
fem. *die* **Frau**	the woman	*die* **Frauen**
neut. *das* **Kind**	the child	*die* **Kinder**

2. Indefinite article (a/an):

masc. *ein* **Zug**	a train
fem. *eine* **Reise**	a trip
neut. *ein* **Flugzeug**	a plane

3. Declension: See under nouns below.

Nouns

1. All nouns are written with a capital letter.

2. **Declension:** According to their use in the sentence, German nouns change their endings. Since articles and modifying adjectives undergo related changes, the tables below show the declension of all three parts of speech.

	masc. sing.	masc. plur.
subject	**der reiche Mann**	**die reichen Männer**
possessive	**des reichen Mannes**	**der reichen Männer**
direct object	**den reichen Mann**	**die reichen Männer**
indirect object	**dem reichen Mann**	**den reichen Männern**

	fem. sing.	fem. plur.
subject	**die schöne Frau**	**die schönen Frauen**
possessive	**der schönen Frau**	**der schönen Frauen**
direct object	**die schöne Frau**	**die schönen Frauen**
indirect object	**der schönen Frau**	**den schönen Frauen**

	neuter sing.	neuter plur.
subject	**das kleine Kind**	**die kleinen Kinder**
possessive	**des kleinen Kindes**	**der kleinen Kinder**
direct object	**das kleine Kind**	**die kleinen Kinder**
indirect object	**dem kleinen Kind**	**den kleinen Kindern**

Adjectives

1. See above. However, the declensions shown are for an adjective used in conjunction with the definite article. Different endings are used for adjectives with the indefinite article or without an article.

2. As can be seen from the above, the position of adjectives within the sentence is similar to English usage.

3. **Demonstrative adjectives:**

	masc.	fem.	neut.	plur.
this	**dieser**	**diese**	**dieses**	**diese**
that	**jener**	**jene**	**jenes**	**jene**

4. **Possessive adjectives:** These agree in number and gender with the noun they modify, i.e., with the thing possessed and not the possessor. They are declined like **der, die, das**.

Note that **Ihr** meaning "your" in the polite form is capitalized.

	masc. or neut.	fem. or plur.
my	**mein**	**meine**
your	**dein**	**deine**
his / its	**sein**	**seine**
her	**ihr** –	**ihre**
our	**unser**	**unsere**
your	**euer**	**eure**
their	**ihr**	**ihre**
your (pol.)	**Ihr**	**Ihre**

5. **Comparatives and superlatives:** These are formed by adding
-er (-r) and **-est (-st)** respectively, very often together with
an *Umlaut*

alt (old)	**kurz** (short)
älter (older)	**kürzer** (shorter)
ältest (oldest)	**kürzest** (shortest)

They are regularly declined:

ein längeres Kleid a longer dress
der kürzeste Weg the shortest way

Adverbs

Many adjectives are used in their undeclined form as adverbs.

schnell quick, quickly
gut good, well

There are a few irregularities:

glücklich – glücklicherweise happy–happily
anders differently
besonders especially
gleichfalls as well, (the) same

Viel indicates quantity and **sehr** intensity:

Er arbeitet viel. He works a lot.
Er ist sehr müde. He's very tired.

GRAMMAR

Personal pronouns

	subject	direct object	indirect object
I	ich	mich	mir
you	du	dich	dir
he	er	ihn	ihm
she	sie	sie	ihr
it	es	es	ihm
we	wir	uns	uns
you	ihr	euch	euch
they	sie	sie	ihnen
you	Sie	Sie	Ihnen

Note: There are two forms for "you" in German: **du** (plur.: **ihr**) is used when talking to relatives, close friends and children (and between young people); **Sie** is used in all other cases. **Sie** is written with a capital **S**. The verb has the same form as that of the 3rd person plural.

Verbs

Here we are concerned only with the infinitive, the present tense, and the imperative.

Learn these two important **auxiliary verbs:**

sein (to be)

ich bin (I am)
du bist (you are)
er, sie, es ist (he, she, it is)
wir sind (we are)
ihr seid (you are)
sie sind (they are)
Sie sind (you are)

haben (to have)

ich habe (I have)
du hast (you have)
er, sie, es hat (he, she, it has)
wir haben (we have)
ihr habt (you have)
sie haben (they have)
Sie haben (you have)

The infinitive of practically all verbs ends in **-en**. Here are the endings for the present tense:

ich liebe   I love
du liebst   you love
er, sie, es liebt   he, she, it loves
wir lieben   we love
ihr liebt   you love
sie, Sie lieben   they, you love

Here are four useful irregular verbs in the present tense:

	können (to be able)	gehen (to go)	sehen (to see)	tun (to do)
ich	kann	gehe	sehe	tue
du	kannst	gehst	siehst	tust
er / sie / es	kann	geht	sieht	tut
wir	können	gehen	sehen	tun
ihr	könnt	geht	seht	tut
sie / Sie	können	gehen	sehen	tun

For both regular and irregular verbs, the **imperative** is formed by reversing the order of the verb and the personal pronoun.

Gehen wir!	Let's go!
Gehen Sie!	Go!

Negatives

Negatives are formed with **nicht**.

Er ist nicht hier.	He is not here.

Questions

These are formed by inverting the subject and the verb (putting the verb first, the subject second).

Sprechen Sie Englisch?	Do you speak English?

GRAMMAR

Guide to pronunciation

This and the following chapter are intended to make you familiar with the phonetic transcription we have devised and to help you get used to the sounds of German.

As a minimum vocabulary for your trip, we've selected a number of basic words and phrases under the title "Some Basic Expressions" (pages 15–21).

You'll find the pronunciation of the German letters and sounds explained below, as well as the symbols we're using for them in the transcriptions.

The imitated pronunciation should be read as if it were English; the symbols for sounds that don't exist in English should, however, be pronounced as described in the appropriate section of the following guide. Of course, the sounds of any two languages are never exactly the same; but if you follow carefully the indications supplied here, you'll have no difficulty in reading our transcriptions in such a way as to make yourself understood.

In the transcriptions, letters shown in bold print should be read with more stress (louder) than the others.

Consonants

Letter	Approximate pronunciation	Symbol	Example	
f, h, k, l, m, n, p, t, x	normally pronounced as in English			
b	1) at the end of a word or between a vowel and a consonant like **p** in up	p	**ab**	ahp
	2) elsewhere as in English	b	**bis**	biss
c	1) before **e**, **i**, **ö** and **ä**, like **ts** in hits	ts	**Celsius**	**ts**ehlzeeuss

	2) elsewhere like c in cat	k	**Café**	kah**fay**
ch	1) after back vowels (e.g. **ah**, **o**, **oo**) like **ch** in Scottish lo**ch**, otherwise more like **h** in huge	kh	**doch**	dokh
	2) sometimes, especially before s, like **k** in **k**it	k	**Wachs**	vahks
d	1) at the end of a word or between a vowel and a consonant like **t** in ea**t**	t	**Rad**	rart
	2) elsewhere, like **d** in **d**o	d	**durstig**	**door**stikh
g	1) always hard as in **g**o but at the end of a word often more like **ck** in ta**ck**	g k	**gehen** **weg**	**gay**ern vehk
	2) when preceded by **i** at the end of a word like **ch** in Scottish lo**ch**	kh	**billig**	**billikh**
j	like **y** in **y**es	y	**ja**	yar
qu	like **k** followed by **v** in **v**at	kv	**Quark**	kvahrk
r	generally rolled in the back of the mouth	r	**warum**	vah**rum**
s	1) before or between vowels like **z** in **z**oo	z	**sie**	zee
	2) before **p** and **t** at the beginning of a syllable like **sh** in **sh**ut	sh	**spät**	shpait
	3) elsewhere, like **s** in **s**it	s/ss	**es ist**	ehss ist
ß	always like **s** in **s**it	s/ss	**heiß**	highss
sch	like **sh** in **sh**ut	sh	**schnell**	shnehl
tsch	like **ch** in **ch**ip	ch	**deutsch**	doych
tz	like **ts** in hi**ts**	ts	**Platz**	plahts
v	like **f** in **f**or	f	**vier**	feer
w	like **v** in **v**ice	v	**wie**	vee
z	like **ts** in hi**ts**	ts	**zeigen**	**tsigh**gern

PRONUNCIATION

Vowels

In Germany, vowels are generally long when followed by **h** or by one consonant and short when followed by two or more consonants.

a	1) short like **u** in cut	ah	**hat**	haht
	2) long like **a** in car	ar*	**Abend**	arbernt
ä	1) short like **e** in let	eh	**Lärm**	lehrm
	2) long like **ai** in hair	ai	**spät**	shpait
e	1) short like **e** in let	eh	**sprechen**	shprehkhern
	2) long like **a** in late	ay	**gehen**	gayern
	3) in unstressed syllables it's generally pronounced like **er** in other	er*	**bitte** **geben**	bitter gaybern
i	1) short like **i** in hit	i	**bis**	biss
	2) long like **ee** in meet	ee	**ihm**	eem
ie	like **ee** in bee	ee	**hier**	heer
o	1) short like **o** in got	o	**voll**	fol
	2) long like **o** in note	oa	**ohne**	oaner
ö	like **ur** in fur (long or short)	ur*	**können**	kurnern
u	1) short like **oo** in foot	u	**Nuß**	nuss
	2) long like **oo** in moon	oo	**gut**	goot
ü	like French **u** in une; no English equivalent. Round your lips and try to say **ea** as in mean	ew	**über**	ewber
y	like German **ü**	ew	**Symphonie**	zewmfoanee

Diphthongs

ai, ay, ei, ey	like **igh** in high	igh	**mein**	mighn
au	like **ow** in now	ow	**auf**	owf
äu, eu	like **oy** in boy	oy	**neu**	noy

* The r should not be pronounced when reading this transcription.

PRONUNCIATION

Some basic expressions

Yes.	**Ja.**	yar
No.	**Nein.**	nighn
Please.	**Bitte.**	bitter
Thank you.	**Danke.**	dahngker
Thank you very much.	**Vielen Dank.**	feelern dahnk
That's all right.	**Gern geschehen.**	gehrn gershayern
You're welcome.	**Bitte.**	bitter

Greetings

Good morning.	**Guten Morgen.**	gootern morgern
Good afternoon.	**Guten Tag.**	gootern targ
Good evening.	**Guten Abend.**	gootern arbernt
Good night.	**Gute Nacht.**	gooter nahkht
Good-bye.	**Auf Wiedersehen.**	owf veederrzayern
See you later.	**Bis bald.**	biss bahlt
This is Mr...	**Das ist Herr...**	dahss ist hehr
This is Mrs...	**Das ist Frau...**	dahss ist frow
This is Miss...	**Das ist Fräulein...**	dahss ist froylighn
How do you do?	**Wie geht es Ihnen?**	vee gayt ehss eenern
I'm very pleased to meet you.	**Sehr erfreut.**	zayr ehrfroyt
How are you?	**Wie geht's?**	vee gayts
Very well, thanks. And you?	**Danke, gut. Und Ihnen?**	dahngker goot, unt eenern
How's it going?	**Wie steht's?**	vee shtayts

Excuse me. (I didn't hear).	**Wie bitte?**	vee **bitter**
Excuse me. (May I get past?)	**Gestatten Sie?**	ger**shtah**tern zee
That's all right.	**Bitte.**	bitter
I beg your pardon.	**Verzeihung. Wie bitte?**	fehr**tsigh**ung, vee **bitter**

Questions

Where?	**Wo?**	voa
Where is...?	**Wo ist...?**	voa ist
Where are...?	**Wo sind...?**	voa zint
When?	**Wann?**	vahn
What?	**Was?**	vahss
How?	**Wie?**	vee
How much?	**Wieviel?**	vee**feel**
How many?	**Wieviele?**	vee**feeler**
Who?	**Wer?**	vayr
Why?	**Warum?**	vah**rum**
Which?	**Welche? (Welcher/Welches)**	**vehl**kher (**vehl**kherr/**vehl**kherss)
What do you call this in German?	**Wie heißt das auf Deutsch?**	vee highst dahss owf doych
What do you call these in German?	**Wie heißen diese auf Deutsch?**	vee **high**ssern **dee**zer owf doych
What does this mean?	**Was bedeutet das?**	vahss ber**doy**tert dahss
Do you speak English?	**Sprechen Sie Englisch?**	**shpreh**khern zee **ehng**lish
I don't speak much German.	**Ich spreche kaum Deutsch.**	ikh **shpreh**kher kowm doych

Could you speak more slowly?	**Könnten Sie bitte langsamer sprechen?**	kurntern zee bitter lahngzahmerr shprehkhern
Could you repeat that?	**Könnten Sie das bitte wiederholen?**	kurntern zee dahss bitter veederrhoalern
Please write it down.	**Schreiben Sie es bitte auf.**	shrighbern zee ehss bitter owf
Can you translate this for me?	**Könnten Sie mir das übersetzen?**	kurntern zee meer dahss ewberrzehtsern
Can you translate this for us?	**Könnten Sie uns das übersetzen?**	kurntern zee uns dahss ewberrzehtsern
Please point to the phrase in the book.	**Bitte zeigen Sie mir den Satz im Buch.**	bitter tsighgern zee meer dayn zahts im bookh
Just a minute. I'll see if I can find it in this book.	**Einen Augenblick bitte, ich schaue mal im Buch nach ob ich ihn finde.**	ighnern owgernblik bitter ikh shower marl im bookh narkh op ikh een finder
I understand.	**Ich verstehe.**	ikh fehrshtayer
I don't understand.	**Ich verstehe nicht.**	ikh fehrshtayer nikht
Do you understand?	**Verstehen Sie?**	fehrshtayern zee

Can...

Can I have...?	**Kann ich... haben?**	kahn ikh... harbern
Can we have...?	**Können wir... haben?**	kurnern veer... harbern
Can you show me...?	**Können Sie mir... zeigen?**	kurnern zee meer... tsighgern
I can't.	**Leider nicht.**	lighderr nikht
Can you tell me...?	**Können Sie mir sagen...?**	kurnern zee meer zargern
Can you help me?	**Können Sie mir helfen?**	kurnern zee meer hehlfern

| Can I help you? | **Kann ich Ihnen helfen?** | kahn ikh **ee**nern **heh**lfern |
| Can you direct me to...? | **Können Sie mir den Weg zu...zeigen?** | kurnern zee meer dayn vayg tsu...**tsigh**gern |

Wanting...

I'd like...	**Ich hätte gern...**	ikh **heh**ter gehrn
We'd like...	**Wir hätten gern...**	veer **heh**tern gehrn
What do you want?	**Was wünschen Sie?**	vahss **vewn**shern zee
Give me...	**Geben Sie mir...**	**gay**bern zee meer
Give it to me.	**Geben Sie es mir.**	**gay**bern zee ehss meer
Bring me...	**Bringen Sie mir...**	**bring**ern zee meer
Bring it to me.	**Bringen Sie es mir.**	**bring**ern zee ehss meer
Show me...	**Zeigen Sie mir...**	**tsigh**gern zee meer
Show it to me.	**Zeigen Sie es mir.**	**tsigh**gern zee ehss meer
I'm looking for...	**Ich suche...**	ikh **zook**her
I'm hungry.	**Ich bin hungrig.**	ikh bin **hung**rikh
I'm thirsty.	**Ich bin durstig.**	ikh bin **doors**tikh
I'm tired.	**Ich bin müde.**	ikh bin **mew**der
I'm lost.	**Ich habe mich verirrt.**	ikh **har**ber mikh feh**reert**
It's important.	**Es ist wichtig.**	ehss ist **vikh**tikh
It's urgent.	**Es ist dringend.**	ehss ist **dring**ernt
Hurry up!	**Beeilen Sie sich bitte.**	be**righ**lern zee zikh **bit**ter

It is/There is...

It is...	**Es ist...**	ehss ist
Is it...?	**Ist es...?**	ist ehss
It isn't...	**Es ist nicht...**	ehss ist nikht
Here it is.	**Hier ist es.**	heer ist ehss
Here they are.	**Hier sind sie.**	heer zint zee
There it is.	**Dort ist es.**	dort ist ehss
There they are.	**Dort sind sie.**	dort zint zee
There is/are...	**Es gibt...**	ehss gipt
Is there/Are there...?	**Gibt es...?**	gipt ehss
There isn't/aren't...	**Es gibt nicht...**	ehss gipt nikht
There isn't/aren't any.	**Es gibt keinen (keine).**	ehss gipt **kigh**nern (**kigh**ner)

It's...

big/small	**groß/klein**	groass/klighn
quick/slow	**schnell/langsam**	shnehl/**lahng**zahm
early/late	**früh/spät**	frew/shpait
cheap/expensive	**billig/teuer**	billikh/**toy**err
near/far	**nah/weit**	nar/vight
hot/cold	**heiß/kalt**	highss/kahlt
full/empty	**voll/leer**	fol/layr
heavy/light	**schwer/leicht**	shvayr/lighkht
open/shut	**offen/geschlossen**	offern/ger**shlos**sern
right/wrong	**richtig/falsch**	**rikh**tikh/fahlsh
old/new	**alt/neu**	ahlt/noy
old/young	**alt/jung**	ahlt/yung
next/last	**nächste/letzte**	**nehkh**ster/**lehts**ter
beautiful/ugly	**schön/häßlich**	shurn/**hehs**likh

free (vacant)	**frei (leer)**	frigh (layr)
occupied	**besetzt**	berzehtst
good/bad	**gut/schlecht**	goot/shlehkht
better/worse	**besser/schlechter**	behsserr/shlehkhterr
here/there	**hier/dort**	heer/dort
now/then	**jetzt/dann**	yehtst/dahn

Quantities

a little/lot	**ein wenig/eine Menge**	ighn vaynikh/ighner mehnger
much/many	**viel/viele**	feel/feeler
more/less (than)	**mehr/weniger (als)**	mayr/vaynigerr (ahlss)
enough/too	**genug/zu (viel)**	gernoog/tsoo (feel)
some (any)	**einige**	ighniger

A few prepositions and some more useful words

at	**an/bei**	ahn/bigh
on	**an/auf**	ahn/owf
in	**in**	in
to	**zu**	tsoo
from	**von**	fon
inside	**drinnen**	drinnern
outside	**draußen**	drowssern
for	**für**	fewr
after	**nach**	nahkh
before	**vor**	foar
with	**mit**	mit
without	**ohne**	oaner

through	**durch**	doorkh
towards	**in Richtung auf**	in rikhtung owf
until	**bis**	biss
during	**während**	vairernt
and	**und**	unt
or	**oder**	oaderr
not	**nicht**	nikht
nothing	**nichts**	nikhts
none	**kein**	kighn
very	**sehr**	zayr
too (also)	**auch**	owkh
soon	**bald**	bahlt
perhaps	**vielleicht**	feelighkht

Arrival

You've arrived. Whether you've come by train, ship or plane, you'll have to go through passport and customs formalities. (For car/border control, see page 146.)

There's certain to be somebody around who speaks English. That's why we're making this a brief section. What you really want is to be off to your hotel in the shortest possible time. And here are the steps to get these formalities out of the way quickly.

Passport control

Here's my passport.	**Hier ist mein Paß.**	heer ist mighn pahss
I'll be staying…	**Ich werde…bleiben.**	ikh vayrder… blighbern
a few days	**ein paar Tage**	ighn parr targer
a week	**eine Woche**	ighner vokher
two weeks	**zwei Wochen**	tsvigh vokhern
a month	**einen Monat**	ighnern moanart
I don't know yet.	**Ich weiß noch nicht.**	ikh vighss nokh nikht
I'm here on holiday.	**Ich bin auf Urlaub hier.**	ikh bin owf oorlowp heer
I'm here on business.	**Ich bin auf Geschäftsreise hier.**	ikh bin owf gershehftsrighzer heer
I'm just passing through.	**Ich bin nur auf der Durchreise.**	ikh bin noor owf derr doorkhrighzer

If things become difficult:

I'm sorry, I don't understand.	**Es tut mir leid, ich verstehe nicht.**	ehss toot meer light ikh fehrshtayer nikht
Is there anyone here who speaks English?	**Spricht hier jemand Englisch?**	shprikht heer yaymahnt ehnglish

Customs

The chart below shows what you can bring in duty-free (visitors from overseas are allowed greater concessions as regards duty-free cigarettes and tobacco).*

	Cigarettes		Cigars		Tobacco (grams)	Spirits (Liquor) (lit.)		Wine (lit.)
Germany	1) 300	or	75	or	400	1½	and	4
	2) 200	or	50	or	250	1	and	2
Austria	200	or	50	or	250	1	and	2
Switzerland	200	or	50	or	250	1	and	2

1) Travellers originating from a country belonging to E.E.C.
2) Travellers originating from a European country outside E.E.C.

German customs may inquire about tea or coffee, since only a limited quantity of either is admitted duty-free.

At almost all major airports in Europe, an honour system for clearing customs has been adopted. Baggage is often not even opened, although spot checks are a possibility. After collecting your baggage, you've a choice: follow the green arrow if you've nothing to declare. Or leave via a doorway marked with a red arrow if you've items to declare.

ARRIVAL

Anmeldefreie Waren Nothing to declare	Zoll Customs		Zoll Customs	**Anmeldepflichtige Waren** Goods to declare

I've nothing to declare.	**Ich habe nichts zu verzollen.**	ikh harber nikhts tsu fehrtsollern
I've...	**Ich habe...**	ikh harber
a carton of cigarettes	**eine Stange Zigaretten**	ighner shtahnger tsiggahrehtern
a bottle of whisky	**eine Flasche Whisky**	ighner flahsher viskee
a bottle of wine	**eine Flasche Wein**	ighner flahsher vighn

* All allowances subject to change without notice.

Must I pay on this?	**Muß ich dafür Zoll zahlen?**	muss ikh **dah**fewr tsol **tsar**lern
How much?	**Wieviel?**	vee**feel**
It's for my personal use.	**Das ist für meinen persönlichen Gebrauch.**	dahss ist fewr **migh**nern pehr**zurn**likhern ger**browkh**
It's not new.	**Es ist nicht neu.**	ehss ist nikht noy

Ihren Paß, bitte.	Your passport, please.
Haben Sie etwas zu verzollen?	Do you have anything to declare?
Bitte öffnen Sie diese Tasche.	Please open this bag.
Dies ist zollpflichtig.	You'll have to pay duty on this.
Haben Sie noch mehr Gepäck?	Do you have any more luggage?

ARRIVAL

Baggage—Porters

In the absence of porters, you'll find do-it-yourself luggage trolleys at the airport. You might find porters at the railway stations, but they are becoming scarce.

Where are the luggage trolleys?	**Wo sind die Kofferkulis?**	voa zint dee **koffer**kooliss
Porter!	**Gepäckträger!**	ger**pehk**traigerr
Please take these bags.	**Nehmen Sie bitte diese Taschen.**	**nay**mern zee bitter **dee**zer **tah**shern
That's mine.	**Das gehört mir.**	dahss ger**hurrt** meer
That's...	**Das ist...**	dahss ist
my bag	**meine Tasche**	**migh**ner **tah**sher
my luggage	**mein Gepäck**	mighn ger**pehk**
my suitcase	**mein Koffer**	mighn **koffer**r
That...one.	**Dieser...**	**dee**zerr
big/small	**große/kleine**	**groass**er/**kligh**ner
blue/brown	**blaue/braune**	**blow**er/**brown**er

FOR TIPPING, see inside back-cover

Take these bags…	**Bringen Sie dieses Gepäck…**	bringern zee deezers gerpehk
to the bus	**zum Bus**	tsum buss
to the luggage lockers	**zu den Schließ-fächern**	tsoo dayn shleesfehkherrn
to the taxi	**zum Taxi**	tsum tahksi
How much is that?	**Wieviel macht das?**	veefeel mahkht dahss

Changing money

You'll find a bank at most airports and leading railway stations. If it's closed, don't worry. You'll be able to change money at your hotel.

Full details about money and currency exchange are given on pages 134–136.

Where's the nearest currency exchange?	**Wo ist die nächste Wechselstube?**	voa ist dee nehkhster vehkserlshtoober
Can you change these traveller's cheques (checks)?	**Können Sie diese Reiseschecks einlösen?**	kurnern zee deezer righzershehks ighnlurzern
I want to change some…	**Ich möchte einige…wechseln.**	ikh murkhter ighniger… vehkserln
dollars/pounds	**Dollar/Pfund**	dollahr/pfunt
Can you change this into…?	**Können Sie das in…umwechseln?**	kurnern zee dahss in… umvehkserln
German marks	**D-Mark**	day-mahrk
Austrian shillings	**Schilling**	shilling
Swiss francs	**Schweizer Franken**	shvightserr frahnkern
What's the exchange rate?	**Wie ist der Wechselkurs?**	vee ist derr vehkserlkoors

Hotel reservations

Many terminals have a hotel reservation service or tourist information office. You're sure to find someone there who speaks English. There's sometimes a special telephone that connects you to a hotel service or to individual hotels.

FOR NUMBERS, see page 175

Car rental

There are car rental firms at most airports and terminals. It's highly likely that someone there will speak English. But if nobody does, try one of the following:

I'd like a...	Ich möchte...	ikh murkhter
car	einen Wagen	ighnern vargern
small car	einen kleinen Wagen	ighnern klighnern vargern
large car	einen großen Wagen	ighnern groassern vargern
sports car	einen Sportwagen	ighnern shportvargern
I'd like it for...	Ich möchte ihn für...	ikh murkhter een fewr
a day/four days	einen Tag/vier Tage	ighnern targ/feer targer
a week/two weeks	eine Woche/zwei Wochen	ighner vokher/tsvigh vokhern
What's the charge per...?	Wieviel kostet es pro...?	veefeel kostert ehss proa
day/week	Tag/Woche	tark/vokher
Does that include mileage?	Ist das Kilometergeld inbegriffen?	ist dahss killommayterrgehlt inbergriffern
What's the charge per kilometre?	Wieviel kostet es pro Kilometer?	veefeel kostert ehss proa killommayterr
Is petrol (gasoline) included?	Ist das Benzin im Preis inbegriffen?	ist dahss behntseen im prighss inbergriffern
I want full insurance.	Ich möchte eine Vollkaskoversicherung.	ikh murkhter ighner folkahskoafehrzikherrung
What's the deposit?	Wieviel muß ich hinterlegen?	veefeel muss ikh hinterrlaygern
I've a credit card.	Ich habe eine Kreditkarte.	ikh harber ighner krehditkahrter
Here's my driving licence.	Hier ist mein Führerschein.	heer ist mighn fewrerrshighn

Note: In Germany you can drive on your own licence; but check if an international licence is required for other countries you may visit.

FOR SIGHTSEEING, see page 75

ARRIVAL

Taxi

Taxis are in plentyful supply, either cruising the streets or waiting at ranks (usually right beside the station). You can also phone for a taxi wherever you are; numbers are listed on a separate page in the front of the phone books. All taxis have meters. There's a night charge between 10 p.m. and 6 a.m.

Where can I get a taxi?	**Wo finde ich ein Taxi?**	voa **finder** ikh ighn **tahksi**
Please get me a taxi.	**Besorgen Sie mir bitte ein Taxi.**	berzorgern zee meer **bitter** ighn **tahksi**
What's the fare to…?	**Was kostet es bis…?**	vahss **kostert** ehss biss
How far is it to…?	**Wie weit ist es bis…?**	vee vight ist ehss biss
Take me to…	**Bringen Sie mich…**	**bringern** zee mikh
this address	**zu dieser Adresse**	tsu **deezerr** ahdrehsser
the airport	**zum Flughafen**	tsum **floogharfern**
the station	**zum Bahnhof**	tsum barnhoaf
the town centre	**in die Stadtmitte**	in dee **shtahtmitter**
the…Hotel	**zum Hotel…**	tsum **hoatehl**
Turn…at the next corner.	**Biegen Sie an der nächsten Ecke…**	**beegern** zee ahn derr **nehkhstern ehker**
left/right	**links ab/rechts ab**	lingks ahp/rehkhts ahp
Go straight ahead.	**Geradeaus.**	gerrah**derowss**
Please stop here.	**Halten Sie hier, bitte.**	**hahltern** zee heer **bitter**
I'm in a hurry.	**Ich habe es eilig.**	ikh **harber** ehss **ighlikh**
Could you drive more slowly?	**Bitte fahren Sie langsamer.**	**bitter** farrern zee **lahngzahmerr**
Could you help me carry my bags?	**Könnten Sie mir bitte mit meinem Gepäck helfen?**	**kurntern** zee meer **bitter** mit **mighnerm** gerpehk **hehlfern**
Will you wait for me, please?	**Würden Sie bitte auf mich warten?**	**vewrdern** zee **bitter** owf mikh **vahrtern**

ARRIVAL

FOR TIPPING, see inside back-cover

Hotel — Other accommodation

Early reservation and confirmation are essential in most major tourist centres during the high season. Most towns and arrival points have a tourist information office (Fremdenverkehrsbüro—**frehm**dernfehrkayrsbewroa), and that's the place to go if you're stuck without a room.

Schloßhotel
(shloshoatehl)

Over 50 castles and palaces have been converted into hotels in Germany and Austria. They're located in the countryside.

Hotel
(hoatehl)

Hotel; simple or fancy, your room will be spotless. You'll doubtless sleep under a quilt filled with duck or goose down. Before you turn in for the night, place your shoes in the corridor outside your room, and next morning you'll find that a kindly elf has cleaned them. *Hotel garni* means that only a room and breakfast are offered.

Rasthaus
(rahsthowss)

Wayside lodge, motel; most are located just off a motorway (turnpike) or principal route.

Gasthaus/Gasthof
(**gahst**howss/**gahst**hoaf)

An inn

Pension/Fremdenheim
(pehnzioan/**frehm**dernhighm)

A boarding-house; offers full or half board. *Zimmer frei* will tell you there's a room to let, sometimes also in a private home.

Jugendherberge
(**yoo**gernthehrbehrger)

Youth hostel; there are 700 in Germany alone.

Ferienwohnung
(**fehr**iernvoanung)

A furnished flat (apartment) found in holiday resorts; you'll probably have to reserve it in advance. Otherwise, contact the local tourist office.

In this section, we're mainly concerned with the smaller and medium-priced hotels and boarding-houses. You'll have no language difficulties in the luxury and first-class hotels where most of the staff speak English.

FOR CAMPING, see page 89

In the next few pages we consider your requirements—step by step—from arrival to departure. You needn't read through all of it. Just turn to the situation that applies.

Checking in—Reception

My name is...	**Ich heiße...**	ikh highsser
I've a reservation.	**Ich habe reservieren lassen.**	ikh harber rehzerrveerern lahssern
We've reserved two rooms, a single and a double.	**Wir haben zwei Zimmer reservieren lassen – ein Einzelzimmer und ein Doppelzimmer.**	veer harbern tsvigh tsimmerr rehzerrveerern lahssern—ighn ighntserltsimmerr unt ighn dopperltsimmerr
I wrote to you last month.	**Ich habe Ihnen im vergangenen Monat geschrieben.**	ikh harber eenern im fehrgahngernern moanaht gershreebern
Here's the confirmation.	**Hier ist die Bestätigung.**	heer ist dee bershtaitigung
I'd like a...	**Ich hätte gern ein...**	ikh hetter gehrn ighn
single room	**Einzelzimmer**	ighntserltsimmerr
double room	**Doppelzimmer**	dopperltsimmerr
room with twin beds	**Zimmer mit zwei Betten**	tsimmerr mit tsvigh behtern
room with a bath	**Zimmer mit Bad**	tsimmerr mit bart
room with a shower	**Zimmer mit Dusche**	tsimmerr mit doosher
room with a balcony	**Zimmer mit Balkon**	tsimmerr mit bahlkoan
room with a view	**Zimmer mit guter Aussicht**	tsimmerr mit gooterr owssikht
We'd like a room...	**Wir hätten gern ein Zimmer...**	veer hehtern gehrn ighn tsimmerr
in the front	**nach vorn**	nahkh forn
an the back	**nach hinten**	nahkh hintern
facing the sea	**mit Blick aufs Meer**	mit blik owfs mayr
facing the courtyard	**mit Blick auf den Hof**	mit blik owf dayn hoaf
It must be quiet.	**Es muß ruhig sein.**	ehss muss rooikh zighn

Is there...?	Gibt es...?	gipt ehss
air conditioning?	Klimaanlage	kleemahahnlarger
heating	Heizung	hightsung
a radio in the room	Radio im Zimmer	rardio im tsimmerr
a television in the room	Fernsehen im Zimmer	fehrnzayern im tsimmerr
laundry service	einen Wäschedienst	ighnern wehsherdeenst
room service	Zimmerbedienung	tsimmerrberdeenung
hot water	warmes Wasser	vahrmerss vahsserr
running water	fließendes Wasser	fleessernderss vahsserr
a private toilet	eine eigene Toilette	ighner ighgerner toylehter

How much?

What's the price...?	Wieviel kostet es...?	veefeel kostert ehss
per week	pro Woche	proa vokher
per night	pro Nacht	proa nahkht
for bed and breakfast	für Übernachtung mit Frühstück	fewr ewberrnahkhtung mit frewshtewk
excluding meals	ohne Mahlzeiten	oaner marltsightern
for full board	mit Vollpension	mit folpehnzioan
for half board	mit Halbpension	mit hahlppehnzioan
Does that include...?	Ist...inbegriffen?	ist...inbergriffen
breakfast	Frühstück	frewshtewk
meals	Essen	ehssern
service	Bedienung	berdeenung
Value-Added Tax*	Mehrwertsteuer	mayrvayrtshtoyerr
Is there any reduction for children?	Gibt es Ermäßigung für Kinder?	gipt ehss ehrmaissigung fewr kinderr
Do you charge for the baby?	Berechnen Sie etwas für das Baby?	berrehkhnern zee ehtvahss fewr dahss baybee
That's too expensive.	Das ist zu teuer.	dahss ist tsu toyerr
Haven't you anything cheaper?	Haben Sie nichts Billigeres?	harbern zee nikhts billigerrers

*Americans note: a type of sales tax

FOR NUMBERS, see page 175

HOTEL

How long?

We'll be staying…	**Wir bleiben…**	veer **bligh**bern
overnight only	**nur eine Nacht**	noor **ighner** nahkht
a few days	**einige Tage**	**ighniger targer**
a week (at least)	**(mindestens) eine Woche**	(**minder**sterns) **ighner vokher**
I don't know yet.	**Ich weiß noch nicht.**	ikh vighss nokh nikht

Decision

May I see the room?	**Kann ich das Zimmer sehen?**	kahn ikh dahss **tsimmerr zayern**
No, I don't like it.	**Nein, es gefällt mir nicht.**	nighn ehss ger**fehlt** meer nikht
It's too…	**Es ist zu…**	ehss ist tsu
cold/hot	**kalt/warm**	kahlt/vahrm
dark/small	**dunkel/klein**	**dungkerl**/**klighn**
noisy	**laut**	lowt
I asked for a room with a bath.	**Ich wollte ein Zimmer mit Bad.**	ikh **volter** ighn **tsimmerr** mit bart
Do you have anything…?	**Haben Sie etwas…?**	**harbern** zee **eht**vahss
better/bigger	**Besseres/Größeres**	**behsserrers**/**grursserrers**
cheaper/quieter	**Billigeres/Ruhigeres**	**billigerrers**/**rooigerrers**
higher up/lower down	**weiter oben/weiter unten**	**vighterr** oabern/**vighterr untern**
Do you have a room with a better view?	**Haben Sie ein Zimmer mit einer besseren Aussicht?**	**harbern** zee ighn **tsimmerr** mit **ighnerr behsserrern owssikht**
That's fine. I'll take it.	**Das ist gut. Ich nehme es.**	dahss ist goot, ikh **naymer** ehss

Bills

These are usually paid weekly or upon departure if you stay less than a week. Some hotels offer a reduction for infants and children.

FOR DAYS OF THE WEEK, see page 181

HOTEL

Tipping

A service charge (10–15 %) is normally included in the bill, but you can ask:

Is service included ?	**Ist die Bedienung inbegriffen ?**	ist dee berdeenung inbergriffern

It's appropriate to give something extra to bellboys, hat-check attendants, etc., for their services.

Registration

Upon arrival at a hotel or boarding-house you'll be asked to fill in a registration form (*Anmeldeformular*—**ahn**mehlder-formullarr). It asks your name, home address, passport number and further destination. It's almost certain to carry an English translation. If it doesn't, ask the desk-clerk:

What does this mean ?	**Was bedeutet das ?**	vahss berdoytert dahss

The desk-clerk will probably ask you for your passport. He may want to keep it for a while. Don't worry. You'll get it back. He may want to ask you the following questions:

Kann ich Ihren Paß sehen ?	May I see your passport ?
Würden Sie bitte dieses Anmeldeformular ausfüllen ?	Would you mind filling in this registration form ?
Unterschreiben Sie hier, bitte.	Please sign here.
Wie lange bleiben Sie ?	How long will you be staying ?

What's my room number?	**Welche Zimmernummer habe ich ?**	vehlker tsimmerrnummerr harber ikh
Will you have our bags sent up?	**Bitte schicken Sie unser Gepäck hinauf**	bitter shikkern zee unzerr gerpehk hinnowf

FOR TIPPING, see inside back-cover

Service, please

bellboy	**der Hotelpage**	derr hoatehlparzher
maid	**das Zimmermädchen**	dahss tsimmerrmaitkhern
manager	**der Geschäftsführer**	derr gershehftsfewrerr
room service	**der Hausdiener**	derr howsdeenerr
switchboard operator	**die Telephonistin**	dee tehlerfonnistin
waiter	**der Kellner**	derr kehlnerr
waitress	**die Kellnerin/**	dee kehlnerrin/
	Serviererin	sehrveererrin

If you want to address members of the staff, don't say *Herr,
Frau* or *Fräulein,* but use a general introductory phrase such
as:

Excuse me. Could you please...?	**Entschuldigen Sie. Könnten Sie bitte...?**	ehntshuldigern zee. kurntern zee bitter

General requirements

Please ask the maid to come up.	**Bitte schicken Sie das Zimmermädchen herauf.**	bitter shikkern zee dahss tsimmerrmaitkhern hehrowf
Who is it?	**Wer ist da?**	vayr ist dar
Just a minute.	**Einen Augenblick, bitte.**	ighnern owgernblik bitter
Come in!	**Herein!**	hehrighn
The door's open.	**Die Tür ist offen.**	dee tewr ist offern
Where is the bath?	**Wo ist das Bad?**	voa ist dahss bart
Where's the plug for the shaver?	**Wo ist die Steckdose für den Rasierapparat?**	voa ist dee shtehkdoazer fewr dayn rahzeerahpahraht
What's the voltage here?	**Welche Stromspannung haben Sie hier?**	vehlkher shtroamshpahnung harbern zee heer
Can we have breakfast in our room?	**Können wir im Zimmer frühstücken?**	kurnern veer im tsimmer frewshtewkern

I'd like to leave this in your safe.	Ich möchte dies gern in Ihrem Tresor lassen.	ikh murkhter deess gehrn in eererm trehzoar lahssern
May I have a/an/some...?	Kann ich...haben?	kahn ikh... harbern
ashtray	einen Aschenbecher	ighnern ahshernbehkherr
bath towel	ein Badetuch	ighn bardertookh
(extra) blanket	eine (extra) Decke	ighner (ekstrar) dehker
envelopes	Briefumschläge	breefumshlaiger
(more) hangers	(noch) einige Kleiderbügel	(nokh) ighniger klighderrbewgerl
ice cubes	Eisstückchen	ighsshtewkkhern
extra pillow	ein extra Kopfkissen	ighn ekstrar kopfkissern
reading-lamp	eine Leselampe	ighner layzerlahmper
soap	Seife	zighfer
writing-paper	Schreibpapier	shrighppahpeer
Where's the...?	Wo ist...?	voa ist
barber's	der Herrenfriseur	derr hehrernfrizurr
bathroom	das Bad	dahss bart
beauty parlour	der Kosmetiksalon	derr kosmaytiksahlong
cocktail lounge	die Bar	dee barr
dining-room	der Speisesaal	derr shpighzerzarl
hairdresser's	der Damenfriseur	derr darmernfrizurr
restaurant	das Restaurant	dahss rehstorrahng
television room	der Fernsehraum	derr fehrnzayrowm
toilet	die Toilette	dee toahlehter

Breakfast

The German breakfast consists of coffee, *Brötchen* (**brurt**khern—crisp buns or rolls, called *Semmeln*—**zeh**merln in Austria and Southern Germany), *Hörnchen* (**hurrn**khern—flaky pastry in the shape of a crescent) and jam.

I'll have a/an/some...	Ich hätte gern...	ikh hehter gehrn
bacon and eggs	Speck und Eier	shpehk unt igherr
eggs	Eier	igherr
boiled egg	ein gekochtes Ei	ighn gerkokhterss igh
soft/medium/hard	weich/ wachsweich/ hartgekocht	vighkh/vahksvighkh/ hahrtgerkokht
fried eggs	Spiegeleier	shpeegerligherr
scrambled eggs	Rühreier	rewrigherr

fruit juice	Fruchtsaft	frukhtsahft
grapefruit	Pampelmusen	pahmperlmoozern
orange	Apfelsinen	ahpferlzeenern
ham and eggs	Schinken und Eier	shinkern unt igherr
jam	Marmelade	mahrmehlarder
marmalade	Apfelsinen-marmelade	ahpferlzeenern-mahrmehlarder
omelet	ein Omelett	ighn omleht
toast	Toast	toast
yoghurt	Joghurt	yoagoort

May I have some...?	Ich hätte gern...	ikh hehter gehrn
hot milk/cold milk	warme Milch/kalte Milch	vahrmer milkh/kahlter milkh
cream/sugar	Sahne/Zucker	zarner/tsukkerr
bread/rolls	Brot/Brötchen	broat/brurtkhern
butter	Butter	butterr
salt/pepper	Salz/Pfeffer	zahlts/pfehferr
coffee/tea	Kaffee/Tee	kahfay/tay
chocolate	Kakao	kahkahoa
lemon/honey	Zitrone/Honig	tsitroaner/hoanikh

Could you bring me a...?	Können Sie mir... bringen?	kurnern zee meer... bringern
plate	einen Teller	ighnern tehlerr
glass/cup	ein Glas/eine Tasse	ighn glarss/ighner tahsser
knife/fork	ein Messer/eine Gabel	ighn mehsserr/ighner garberl
spoon	einen Löffel	ighnern lurferl

Difficulties

The...doesn't work.	...funktioniert nicht.	...funktionneert nikht
air-conditioner	die Klimaanlage	dee kleemarahnlarger
fan	der Ventilator	derr vehntillartoar
heating	die Heizung	dee hightsung
light	das Licht	dahss likht
radio	das Radio	dahss rardio
tap	der Wasserhahn	derr vahsserrharn
toilet	die Toilette	dee toahlehter
ventilator	der Lüfter	derr lewfterr
The wash-basin is clogged.	Das Waschbecken ist verstopft.	dahss vahshbehkern ist fehrshtopft

FOR EATING OUT, see pages 38–64

HOTEL SERVICE

The window is jammed.	**Das Fenster klemmt.**	dahss **fehns**terr klehmt
The blind is stuck.	**Die Jalousie klemmt.**	dee zhahloo**zee** klehmt
These aren't my shoes.	**Dies sind nicht meine Schuhe.**	deess zint nikht **migh**ner **shoo**er
This isn't my laundry.	**Das ist nicht meine Wäsche.**	dahss ist nikht **migh**ner **veh**sher
There's no hot water.	**Es kommt kein warmes Wasser.**	ehss komt kighn **vahr**mers **vahs**serr
I've lost my watch.	**Ich habe meine Uhr verloren.**	ikh **har**ber **migh**ner oor fehr**loar**ern
I've left my key in my room.	**Ich habe meinen Schlüssel im Zimmer gelassen.**	ikh **har**ber **migh**nern **shlews**serl im **tsim**merr ger**lahs**sern
The...is broken.	...**ist kaputt.**	...ist kah**put**
bulb	**die Glühbirne**	dee **glew**beerner
lamp	**die Lampe**	dee **lahm**per
plug	**die Steckdose**	dee **shtehk**doazer
shutter	**das Rollo**	dahss rolloa
switch	**der Schalter**	derr **shahl**terr
window shade	**die Sonnenblende**	dee **sonnern**blehnder
Can you get it repaired?	**Können Sie es reparieren lassen?**	**kurn**ern zee ehss rehpah**ree**rern **lahs**sern

Telephone—Mail—Callers

Can you get me Vienna 123456?	**Können Sie mich mit Wien 123456 verbinden?**	**kurn**ern zee mikh mit veen 123456 fehr**bin**dern
Did anyone telephone me?	**Hat mich jemand angerufen?**	haht mikh **yay**mahnt **ahn**gerroofern
Do you have stamps?	**Haben Sie Briefmarken?**	**har**bern zee **breef**mahrkern
Would you please mail this for me?	**Könnten Sie das bitte für mich aufgeben?**	**kurn**tern zee dahss **bit**ter fewr mikh **owf**gaybern
Are there any messages for me?	**Hat jemand für mich eine Nachricht hinterlassen?**	haht **yay**mahnt fewr mikh **igh**ner **nark**rikht **hinterr**lahssern

FOR POST OFFICE AND TELEPHONE, see pages 137–141

Checking out

May I please have my bill?	**Kann ich bitte die Rechnung haben?**	kahn ikh **bi**tter dee **reh**khnung **har**bern
I'm leaving early tomorrow. Please have my bill ready.	**Ich reise morgen früh ab. Bereiten Sie bitte meine Rechnung vor.**	ikh **righ**zer **mor**gern frew ahp. berrightern zee **bi**tter **migh**ner **reh**khnung foar
We'll be checking out around noon.	**Wir fahren gegen Mittag ab.**	veer **fa**rrern **gay**gern **mit**tark ahp
I must leave at once.	**Ich muß sofort abreisen.**	ikh muss zoa**fort** **ahp**righzern
Is everything included?	**Ist alles inbegriffen?**	ist **ah**lerss **in**bergriffern
You've made a mistake in this bill, I think.	**Ich glaube, Sie haben sich verrechnet.**	ikh **glow**ber zee **har**bern zikh fehr**reh**khnert
Can you get us a taxi?	**Können Sie uns ein Taxi bestellen?**	**kur**nern zee uns ighn **tah**ksi ber**shteh**lern
When's the next train to Hamburg?	**Wann geht der nächste Zug nach Hamburg?**	vahn gayt derr **naikh**ster tsoog nakh **hahm**boorg
plane/bus	**das Flugzeug/der Bus**	dahss **floog**tsoyg/derr buss
Would you send someone to bring down our baggage?	**Würden Sie bitte unser Gepäck hinunterbringen lassen?**	**vewr**dern zee **bi**tter **un**zerr ger**pehk** hi**nun**terrbringern **lah**ssern
We're in a great hurry.	**Wir haben es sehr eilig.**	veer **har**bern ehss zayr **igh**likh
Here's the forwarding address.	**Hier ist meine Nachsendeadresse.**	heer ist **migh**ner **narkh**zehnderahdrehsser
You have my home address.	**Sie haben meine Heimatadresse.**	zee **har**bern **migh**ner **high**mahtahdrehsser
It's been a very enjoyable stay.	**Es war ein sehr angenehmer Aufenthalt.**	ehss varr ighn zayr **ahn**gernaymerr **owf**ehnthahlt
I hope we'll come again sometime.	**Ich hoffe, daß wir mal wiederkommen.**	ikh **hof**fer dahss veer marl **vee**derrkommern

FOR TAXI, see page 27

HOTEL SERVICE

Eating out

There are many types of places where you can eat and drink in Germany, Austria and Switzerland.

Bierhalle
(beerhahler)

Beer hall; besides beer served from huge barrels, you'll also be able to order hot dishes, sausages, salads and pretzels. The best-known beer halls are those in Munich which has a giant beer festival *(Oktoberfest)* annually in late September.

Café
(kahfay)

Coffee shop; besides coffee, you'll be able to get pastries, snacks and drinks. Often a *Konditorei* (pastry shop) will have a salon for coffee and pastries. A *café* is a *Kaffeehaus* in Austria and sometimes called a *Tea-Room* in Switzerland. There's a small dance floor in a *Tanzcafé*.

Gasthaus
(gahsthowss)

Inn; usually in the country, it offers home-cooking and a folksy atmosphere. Other words for *Gasthaus* are *Gasthof* and *Beisel* in Austria.

Milchbar
(milkhbarr)

A bar serving mainly plain and flavoured milk drinks with pastries. Also called a *Milchstübl*.

Raststätte
(rahstshtaiter)

Roadside restaurant; also called a *Rasthof* in Austria; it's usually found on a motorway (turnpike). Lodging and service-station facilities are on the premises.

Restaurant
(rehstoarahng)

These are generally found only in urban areas. Menus often cater to foreign visitors as well as offering numerous local specialities.

Schnellimbiß
(shnehlimbiss)

Snack bar; the English term is also seen. The principal fare is beer and sausages. A sausage stand *(Würstchenstand)* is often quite similar.

Weinstube
(vighnstoober)

A cozy type of restaurant found in wine-producing districts where you can sample new wine with simple hot dishes and snacks. In Austria, it's called a *Heuriger* and is identified by a wreath hanging over the portal.

Lunch (*das Mittagessen*—dahss **mit**tahgehssern) is generally served from 11.30 a.m. until 2 p.m.

Dinner (*das Abendessen*—dahss **ar**berntehssern) is served from 6.30 to 8.30 p.m., in large restaurants to 10 or 11 p.m. After this it's usually a case of cold snacks or hot sausages only.

Eating habits

Most restaurants display a menu *(Speisekarte)* outside. Besides the à la carte menu, they'll usually offer one or more set menus *(Menü* or *Gedeck)*. Value-added tax—a type of sales tax *(Mehrwertsteuer* or *Mwst)*—and a service charge *(Bedienung)* are usually included. The tip is up to you. You may want to leave some small change.

A *Tagesgericht* (**tar**gersgehrikht—the day's special) usually offers you a good meal at a fair price.

Terms on the menu like *Spezialität des Hauses, Nach Art des Hauses* or *Unser Küchenchef empfiehlt* will tell you that these items on the menu are specialities of the house.

Was nehmen Sie?	What would you like?
Ich empfehle Ihnen...	I recommend...
Was trinken Sie?	What would you like to drink?
Möchten Sie...?	Do you want...?
...haben wir nicht.	We haven't got...

Hungry

I'm hungry/I'm thirsty.	**Ich habe Hunger/ Ich habe Durst.**	ikh **har**ber hunger/ikh **har**ber doorst
Can you recommend a good restaurant?	**Können Sie mir ein gutes Restaurant empfehlen?**	kurnern zee meer ighn **goo**terss rehstoa**rahng** ehmp**fay**lern
Is there an inexpensive restaurant around here?	**Gibt es in der Nähe ein preiswertes Restaurant?**	gibt ehss in derr **nai**er ighn **prighs**vehrterss rehstoa**rahng**

FOR BREAKFAST, see page 34

If you want to be sure of getting a table in well-known restaurants, it may be better to telephone in advance.

I'd like to reserve a table for 4.	**Ich möchte einen Tisch für 4 Personen reservieren lassen.**	ikh murkhter ighnern tish fewr 4 pehrzoanern rehzehrveerern lahssern
We'll come at 8.	**Wir kommen um 8 Uhr.**	veer kommern oom 8 oor

Asking and ordering

Good evening. I'd like a table for 3.	**Guten Abend. Ich hätte gern einen Tisch für 3 Personen.**	gootern arbernt. ikh hehter gehrn ighnern tish fewr 3 pehrzoanern
Could we have a table...?	**Können wir einen Tisch ... haben?**	kurnern veer ighnern tish ... harbern
in the corner	**in der Ecke**	in derr ehker
by the window	**am Fenster**	ahm fehnsterr
outside	**im Freien**	im frighern
on the terrace	**auf der Terrasse**	owf derr tehrahsser
Where are the toilets?	**Wo ist die Toilette?**	voa ist dee toaahlehter
May I please have the menu?	**Kann ich bitte das Menü haben?**	kahn ikh bitter dahss maynew harbern
What's this?	**Was ist das?**	vahss ist dahss
Do you have...?	**Haben Sie...?**	harbern zee...?
a set menu	**ein Tagesmenü**	ighn targersmaynew
local dishes	**Spezialitäten**	shpaytsiahlitaitern
Is service included?	**Ist die Bedienung inbegriffen?**	ist dee berdeenung inbergriffern
Could we have (a/an) ..., please?	**Könnten wir bitte ... haben?**	kurntern veer bitter ... harbern
ashtray	**einen Aschenbecher**	ighnern ashernbehkherr
(another) chair	**(noch) einen Stuhl**	(nokh) ighnern shtool
glass	**ein Glas**	ighn glarss
knife	**ein Messer**	ighn mehsserr
napkin	**eine Serviette**	ighner sehrvyehter
plate	**einen Teller**	ighnern tehlerr
serviette	**eine Serviette**	ighner sehrvyehter
spoon	**einen Löffel**	ighnern lurferl
toothpick	**einen Zahnstocher**	ighnern tsarnshtokherr

FOR COMPLAINTS, see page 55

EATING OUT

I'd like a/an/ some...	Ich hätte gern...	ikh **hehter** gehrn
aperitif	einen Aperitif	**ighnern** ahpehritt**eef**
appetizer	eine Vorspeise	**ighner foarsh**pighzer
beer	ein Bier	**ighn** beer
bread	etwas Brot	**ehtvahss** broat
butter	etwas Butter	**ehtvahss butterr**
cabbage	Kohl	koal
cheese	etwas Käse	**ehtvass** kaizer
chips	Pommes frites	pom frit
coffee	einen Kaffee	**ighnern** kahfay
dessert	einen Nachtisch	**ighnern** nahkhtish
fish	ein Fischgericht	ighn **fish**gayrikht
french fries	Pommes frites	pom frit
fruit	etwas Obst	**ehtvass** oapst
game	Wild	vilt
ice-cream	ein Eis/eine Glace	ighn **ighss/ighner**
	(Switzerland)	**glah**sser
ketchup	Tomatenketchup	toamart**ern**kehtshap
lemon	etwas Zitrone	**ehtvahss** tsitroaner
lettuce	Kopfsalat	**kopf**zahlart
meat	Fleisch	flighsh
milk	Milch	milkh
mineral water	ein Mineralwasser	ighn minnehr**arlvah**sser
mustard	etwas Senf	**ehtvahss** zehnf
oil	etwas Öl	**ehtvahss** url
olive oil	etwas Olivenöl	**ehtvahss** oalee**vern**url
pepper	etwas Pfeffer	**ehtvahss pfeff**err
potatoes	Kartoffeln	kahr**toff**erln
poultry	Geflügel	geh**flewg**erl
rice	Reis	righss
roll	ein Brötchen	ighn **brurt**khern
salad	Salat	zah**lart**
salt	etwas Salz	**ehtvahss** zahltss
sandwich	ein Sandwich	ighn **sehnd**vitsh
seafood	Meeresfrüchte	**may**rersfrewkhter
seasoning	etwas Würze	**ehtvahss vewrt**ser
soup	eine Suppe	**ighner** zupper
spaghetti	Spaghetti	**shpah**gehtee
starter	eine Vorspeise	**ighner foar**spighzer
sugar	etwas Zucker	**ehtvahss** tsukkerr
tea	einen Tee	**ighnern** tay
vegetables	Gemüse	geh**mewz**er
vinegar	etwas Essig	**ehtvahss ehss**ikh
(iced) water	(Eis-)Wasser	(**ighss-**)**vah**sserr
wine	(einen) Wein	(**ighnern**)vighn

What's on the menu?

Our menu is presented according to courses. Under each of the headings you'll find an alphabetical list of dishes that might be offered on a German menu with their English equivalent. You can also show the book to the waiter. If you want some fruit, for instance, show him the appropriate list and let him point at what's available. Use pages 40 and 41 for ordering in general.

Here then is our guide to good eating and drinking. Turn to the section you want.

Obviously, you're not going to go through every course. If you've had enough say:

Nothing more, thanks. **Nichts mehr, danke.**   nikhtss mayr **dahngker**

One could hardly go away hungry from a German table. Meals are rich and satisfying and are often reminiscent of our homecooking. You'll enjoy the succulent sausages, tender potroasted meats, smoked pork, dark breads, rich gravies and sumptuous desserts.

EATING OUT

Appetizers

If you feel like something to whet your appetite, choose carefully, for the German appetizer can be filling.

I'd like an appetizer.	**Ich hätte gern eine Vorspeise.**	ikh **heh**ter gehrn **ig**hner **foarsh**pighzer
What do you recommend?	**Was würden Sie empfehlen?**	vahss **vewr**dern zee ehm**pfay**lern

Aal	arl	eel
Aal in Gelee	arl in zher**lay**	jellied eel
Appetithäppchen	apeh**teet**hehpkhern	canapés
Artischocken	**ahrt**ishokkern	artichoke
Austern	**ows**terrn	oysters
Bückling	**bew**kling	bloater, kipper
Fleischpastete	**fligsh**pahstayter	meat loaf
Froschschenkel	**frosh**shehnkerl	frog's legs
Gänseleberpastete	**gehn**zerlayberr-pahstayter	pâté, goose liver purée
Hering	**hay**ring	herring
Hummer	**hum**merr	lobster
Käsehäppchen	**kai**zerhehpkhern	cheese sticks
Kaviar	**kar**viahr	caviar
Krabben	**krah**bern	prawn, shrimp
Krebs	krayps	crayfish
Lachs	lahks	salmon
Langusten	lahng**gus**tern	spiny lobster
Makrelen	mah**kray**lern	mackerel
Muscheln	**mush**erln	mussels
Oliven	oa**lee**vern	olives
Pilze	**pilt**ser	mushrooms
Räucheraal	**royk**herrarl	smoked eel
Räucherhering	**royk**herrhayring	smoked herring
Russische Eier	**rus**sisher **igh**err	hard-boiled eggs with mayonnaise
Sardellen	zahr**deh**lern	anchovies
Sardinen	zahr**dee**nern	sardines
Schinken	**shing**kern	ham
roher Schinken	**roa**err **shing**kern	cured ham
gekochter Schinken	geh**kokh**terr **shing**kern	boiled ham
Schnecken	**shneh**kern	snails
Spargelspitzen	**shparr**gerlshpitsern	asparagus tips
Thunfisch	**toon**fish	tunny, tuna
Wurst	**voorst**	sausage
Wurstplatte	**voorst**plahter	assorted cold cuts

German specialities

Bismarckhering (bismahrkhayring)	soused herring with onions
Frisch geräucherte Gänsebrust auf Toast (frish gehroykherrter gehnzerbrust owf toast)	freshly smoked breast of goose on toast
Hoppel-Poppel (hopperl-popperl)	scrambled eggs with diced sausages or bacon
Königinpastete (kurneeginpahstayter)	puff-pastry shell filled with diced meat and mushrooms
Matjeshering (mahtyehshayring)	salted young herring
Matjesfilet nach Hausfrauenart (mahtyehsfeelay nahk howsfrowernahrt)	fillets of herring with apples and onions
Hausgemachte Rehpastete (howsgehmakhkter raypahstayter)	home-made venison meatloaf
Schinkenröllchen mit Spargel (shingkernrurlkhern mit shpahrgerl)	rolled ham with asparagus filling
Strammer Max (strahmer mahkss)	highly spiced minced pork served with eggs and onions

Soup and stew

German soup can be hearty fare and particularly welcome on a cold day. *Eintopf* is a stew and will usually be a meal in itself.

I'd like some soup.	**Ich möchte gerne eine Suppe.**	ikh murkhter gehrner ighner zupper
Aalsuppe	arlzupper	eel soup
Bauernsuppe	bowerrnzupper	cabbage and frankfurter soup
Bohnensuppe	boanernzupper	bean soup with bacon
Bouillon	boolyong	clear soup
Erbsensuppe	ehrpsernzupper	pea soup
Fischsuppe	fishzupper	fish soup
Fischbeuschelsuppe	fishboysherlzupper	fish roe and vegetable soup
Fridattensuppe	freedahtternzupper	broth with pancake strips

Frühlingssuppe	frewlingszupper	spring vegetable soup
Grießnockerlsuppe	greesnokkerrlzupper	semolina-dumpling soup
Gulaschsuppe	goolahshzupper	spiced soup of stewed beef
Hühnerbrühe	hewnerrbrewer	chicken broth
Kartoffelsuppe	kahrtofferlzupper	potato soup
(Semmel-) Knödelsuppe	(zehmerl-)knurderlzupper	dumpling soup
Königinsuppe	kurniginzupper	with beef, sour cream and almonds
Kraftbrühe mit Ei	krahftbrewer mit igh	beef consommé with raw egg
Leberknödelsuppe	layberrknurdelzupper	liver-dumpling soup
Linsensuppe	linzernzupper	lentil soup
Nudelsuppe	nooderlzupper	noodle soup
Ochsenschwanzsuppe	oksernshvahntszupper	oxtail soup
Pichelsteiner Eintopf	pikherlshtighnerr ighntopf	meat and vegetable stew
Schildkrötensuppe	shiltkrurternzupper	turtle soup
Serbische Bohnensuppe	zehrbisher boanernzupper	spiced bean soup
Tomatensuppe	toamarternzupper	tomato soup
Zwiebelsuppe	tsveeberlzupper	onion soup

Backerbsensuppe (bahkehrpsernzupper)	broth served with small, round croutons
Basler Mehlsuppe (barslerr maylzupper)	flour soup with grated cheese (Swiss)
Kaltschale/Kalte Obstsuppe (kahltsharler/kahlter oapstzupper)	fruit soup, served chilled, sometimes containing beer or wine
Labskaus (larpskowss)	thick stew of minced and marinated meat with mashed potatoes

Fish and seafood

I'd like some fish.	**Ich hätte gerne Fisch.**	ikh hehter gehrner fish
What kind of seafood do you have ?	**Welche Meeresfrüchte haben Sie ?**	vehlkher mayrersfrewkhter harbern zee
Aal	arl	eel
Austern	owsterrn	oysters
Barsch	barsh	freshwater perch
Brasse/Brachse	brahsser/brahkser	bream

Dorsch	dorsh	a variety of codfish
Fischfrikadellen	fishfrikkahdehlern	fish croquettes
Forelle	forehler	trout
Flunder	flunderr	flounder
Garnelen	gahrnaylern	prawns
Hecht	hehkht	pike
Heilbutt	highlbut	halibut
Hering	hayring	herring
Hummer	hummerr	lobster
Jakobsmuscheln	yarkopsmusherln	scallops
Kabeljau	karberlyow	cod
Karpfen	kahrpfern	carp
Krebs	kraypss	crab
Lachs	lahks	salmon
Languste	lahnggooster	spiny lobster
Makrele	mahkrayler	mackerel
Muscheln	musherln	clams/mussels/ cockles
Neunauge	noynowger	lamprey eel
Rotbarsch	roatbahrsh	red sea-bass
Salm	zahlm	salmon
Schellfisch	shehlfish	haddock
Scholle	sholler	plaice
Seebarsch	zaybahrsh	sea bass
Seebutt	zaybut	brill
Seezunge	zaytsunger	sole
Sprotten	shprottern	sprats
Steinbutt	shtighnbut	turbot
Stint	shtint	smelt
Stör	shturr	sturgeon
Zander	tsahnderr	(giant) pike-perch

Here are some of the ways you may want your fish served:

baked	**gebacken**	gehbahkern
boiled in bouillon	**blau**	blow
fried	**gebraten**	gehbrartern
deep-fried	**im schwimmenden**	im shvimmerndern
	Fett gebacken	feht gehbahkern
grilled	**gegrillt**	gehgrilt
marinated	**mariniert**	mahrinneert
sautéed (in butter)	**(in Butter)**	(in butterr)
	geschwenkt	gehshvehngkt
smoked	**geräuchert**	gehroykhert
steamed	**gedämpft**	gehdehmpft

Meat

Bear in mind that the Germans most often write in one word
what would take us two or more. For example, *Rindszunge* is
Rinds- (beef) and *-zunge* (tongue) or *Kalbsbrust* is breast of
veal. So you may have to look under two entries in the following lists to fully understand what's on the menu.

I'd like some...	Ich hätte gern...	ikh hehter gehrn
beef	**Rindfleisch**	rintflighsh
lamb	**Lammfleisch**	lahmflighsh
pork	**Schweinefleisch**	shvighnerflighsh
veal	**Kalbfleisch**	kahlpflighsh
Bauernomelett	bowerrnomleht	diced bacon and onion omelet
(deutsches) Beefsteak	(doytsherss) beef-stayk	hamburger steak
Beuschel	boysherl	veal lungs, heart, glands with lemon sauce
Bierwurst	beervoorst	beer sausage
Blutwurst	blootvoorst	black pudding (blood sausage)
Bockwurst	bokvoorst	large frankfurter
Bratwurst	brartvoorst	fried sausage
-braten	-brartern	joint, roast
-brust	-brust	breast
Bündnerfleisch	bewndnerrflighsh	cured, dried beef served in paper-thin slices
Eisbein	ighsbighn	pickled pig's knuckle
Faschiertes	fahsheerterss	minced meat
Filetsteak	fillaystayk	beef steak
Fleischkäse	flighshkaize	type of bologna sausage
Frikadellen	frikahdehlern	croquettes
Geschnetzeltes	gehshnehtserlterss	chipped veal served in wine sauce
Geselchtes	gehzehlkhterss	smoked or salted meat usually pork
Gulasch	goolahsh	gulash; chunks of beef stewed in a rich paprika gravy
Hackbraten	hahkbrartern	meatloaf
-herz	-hehrtss	heart

Kasseler Rippenspeer	kahssehlerr rippernshpayr	smoked pork chops
-klößchen	-klursskhern	meatballs
-kotelett	-kotleht	cutlet, chop
Krenfleisch	kraynflighsh	pork, usually brawn, served with shredded vegetables and horseradish
Kutteln	kutterln	tripe
Leber	layberr	liver
Leberkäse	layberrkaizer	type of meatloaf
Nieren	neerern	kidneys
Rippensteak	rippernshtayk	rib steak
Rotwurst	roatvoorst	black pudding (blood sausage)
Rouladen	roolardern	slices of beef or veal filled, rolled and braised (in brown gravy)
Schinken	shingkern	ham
Schlachtplatte	shlahkhtplahter	platter of various sausages and cold meats
Schnitzel	shnitserl	cutlet
Spanferkel	shparnfehrkerl	sucking pig
Speck	shpehk	bacon
Sülze	sewltser	brawn (headcheese)
Wiener Schnitzel	veenerr shnitserl	breaded veal cutlet
-wurst	-voorst	sausage
-zunge	-tsunger	tongue

Here are some hearty dishes you'll certainly want to try:

Bauernschmaus (bowerrnshmowss)	sauerkraut garnished with boiled bacon, smoked pork, sausages, dumplings, potatoes (Austrian)
Berner Platte (behrnerr plahter)	sauerkraut (or green beans) liberally garnished with pork chops, boiled bacon and beef, sausages, tongue and ham (Swiss)
Holsteiner Schnitzel (holshtighnerr shnitserl)	breaded veal cutlet topped with fried egg and usually garnished with pieces of tast, anchovies, mussels, smoked salmon and vegetables
Kohlroulade (koalroolarder)	cabbage leaves stuffed with minced meat
Königsberger Klops (kurnigsbehrgerr klops)	Meatballs in white caper sauce

EATING OUT

How do you like your meat?

baked	gebacken	gehbahkern
boiled	gekocht	gehkokht
braised	geschmort	gehshmoart
broiled	vom Rost	fom roast
fried	(in der Pfanne) gebraten	(een derr pfahner) gehbrartern
grilled	gegrillt	gehgrilt
roasted	(im Ofen) gebraten	(eem oafern) gehbrartern
stewed	gedämpft	gehdehmpft
stuffed	gefüllt	gehfewlt
underdone (rare)	blutig	blootikh
medium	mittel	mitterl
well-done	gut durchgebraten	goot doorchgehbrartern

Game and fowl

Back-	bahk-	fried
Brat-	brart-	roast
-braten	-brartern	joint, roast
Ente	ehnter	duck
Fasan	fahzarn	pheasant
Gans	gahnss	goose
Hähnchen	hainkhern	chicken
Hase	harzer	hare
-hendl	-hehndl	chicken
gespickter Hirsch	gehshpikterr heersh	larded venison
Huhn	hoon	chicken
Kaninchen	kahneenkhern	rabbit
Kapaun	kahpown	capon
-keule	-koyler	haunch
Masthühnchen	mahsthewnkhern	pullet chicken
Rebhuhn	rehphoon	partridge
Reh	ray	venison
-rücken	-rewkern	saddle
Taube	towber	pigeon, squab
Truthahn	trootharn	turkey
Wachtel	vahkhterl	quail
Wildschwein	viltshvighn	wild boar

If your meal is prepared *nach Jägerart* (in the hunter's style), it's likely sautéed with mushrooms and root vegetables and served in a wine gravy.

EATING OUT

Potatoes, rice and noodles

Brat-	brart-	fried
Butterreis	butterrighss	buttered rice
Curryreis	curreerighss	curried rice
Geröstel	gehrursterl	hashed-brown potatoes
Kartoffel(n)	kahrtofferl(n)	potato(es)
-bälle	-behler	balls
-brei	-brigh	mashed
-klöße	-klursser	dumplings
-puffer	-pufferr	fritters
-kroketten	-kroakehtern	croquettes
Makkaroni	mahkahroanee	macaroni
Nudeln	nooderln	noodles
Pellkartoffeln	pehlkahrtofferln	potatoes boiled in their jackets
Petersilienkartoffeln	payterrzeeliernkahrtofferln	parsleyed potatoes
Pommes frites	pom frit	chips (french fries)
Reis	righss	rice
Röst-	rurst-	fried
Rösti	rurshtee	hashed-brown potatoes
Salzkartoffeln	zahltskahrtofferln	boiled potatoes
Spätzle	shpehtsler	thick noodles
Teigwaren	tighgvarrern	noodles

Vegetables, salads

What vegetables do you recommend?	Welches Gemüse empfehlen Sie?	vehlkherss gehmewzer ehmpfaylern zee
I'd prefer some salad.	Ich nehme lieber Salat.	ikh naymer leeberr zahlart
Auberginen	oaberrzheenern	aubergines (eggplant)
Blumenkohl	bloomernkoal	cauliflower
Bohnen	boanern	beans
grüne/weiße	grewner/wighsser	green/white
Braunkohl	brownkoal	broccoli
Champignons	shahmpinyong	button mushrooms
Chicorée	sheekoaray	endive (chicory)
Endivien	ehndeeviern	chicory (endives)
Erbsen	ehrpsern	peas
Essiggurken	ehssikhgoorkern	gherkins
Essigkren	ehssikhkrayn	prepared horseradish
Fisolen	feesoalern	french (green) beans

Gemüse	geh**mew**zer	vegetables
gemischtes	geh**mish**terss	mixed vegetables
grüner Salat	**grew**nerr **zah**lart	green salad
Gurken	**goor**kern	cucumber
Häuptlsalat	**hoyptl**zahlart	lettuce salad
Karfiol	**kahr**fioal	cauliflower
Karotten	**kah**rottern	carrots
Kohl	koal	cabbage
Kopfsalat	**kopf**zahlart	lettuce salad
Kürbis	**kewr**biss	pumpkin
Lauch	lowkh	leeks
Leipziger Allerlei	**lighpt**seegerr **ah**lerrligh	peas, carrots, asparagus
Mais	mighss	maize (corn)
Meerrettich	**mayr**rehtikh	horseradish
Mohrrüben	**moar**rewbern	carrots
Paradeiser	**pah**rah**digh**zerr	tomatoes
Pfifferlinge	**pfiffer**rlinger	chanterelle mushrooms
Pilze	**pilt**ser	mushrooms
Radieschen	**rah**dees**khern**	radishes
Rosenkohl	**roa**zern**koal**	brussels sprouts
rote Beete/Rüben	**roa**ter **bay**ter/**rew**bern	beetroot
Rotkohl	**roat**koal	red cabbage
Salat	**zah**lart	salad
gemischter	geh**mish**terr	mixed salad
Sauerkraut	**zow**errkrowt	sauerkraut
Schwarzwurzeln	**shvahrts**voortserln	salsify
Sellerie	**zeh**lerree	celery
Spargel	**shparr**gerl	asparagus
Spargelspitzen	**shparr**gerl**shpit**sern	asparagus tips
Spinat	**shpee**nart	spinach
Tomaten	to**mmart**ern	tomatoes
Weißkohl	**vighs**koal	cabbage
Zwiebeln	**tsvee**berln	onions

Vegetables may be served…

boiled	**gekocht**	geh**kokht**
creamed	**-püree**	pew**ray**
diced	**gehackt**	geh**hahkt**
grilled	**gegrillt**	geh**grilt**
stewed	**gedämpft**	geh**dehmpft**

Cheese

Most of the cheese produced in Germany, Austria and Switzerland is mild. Though there's no cheese course like in neighbouring France, you may see *Käseteller* (**kai**zertehlerr) on the menu. This means you'll get a plate of three or four varieties of cheese, doubtless including the renowned *Emmentaler* (**eh**merntarlerr), which we call simply Swiss cheese. Here are other favourite types of cheese:

mild	Allgäuer Bergkäse (like Swiss cheese), Allgäuer Rahmkäse, Altenburger (made of goat's milk), Appenzeller, Edamer, Greyerzer, Kümmelkäse (made with caraway seeds), Quark, Räucherkäse (smoked cheese), Schichtkäse, Sahnekäse, Tilsiter, Topfen, Weißkäse.
sharp	Handkäse, Harzer Käse, Schabzieger.

Fruit

Do you have (fresh) fruit?	Haben Sie (frisches) Obst?	harbern zee (frisherss) oapst
I'd like a fruit cocktail.	Ich hätte gern einen Obstsalat.	ikh hehter gehrn ighnern oapstzahlart

Ananas	ahnahnahss	pineapple
Apfel	ahpferl	apple
Apfelsine	ahpferlzeener	orange
Aprikosen	ahpreekoazern	apricots
Banane	bahnarner	banana
Birne	beerner	pear
Blaubeeren	blowbayrern	bilberries (blueberries)
Brombeeren	brombayrern	blackberries
Datteln	dahterln	dates
Erdbeeren	ehrtbayrern	strawberries
Johannisbeeren	yoahahnisbayrern	currants
Feigen	fighgern	figs
Haselnüsse	harzerlnewsser	hazelnuts
Heidelbeeren	highderlbayrern	bilberries (blueberries)
Himbeeren	himbayrern	raspberries
Kirschen	keershern	cherries
Kokosnuß	kokkosnuss	coconut
Mandarine	mahndahreener	tangerine
Mandeln	mahnderln	almonds
Marillen	marrillern	apricots
Mirabellen	meerahbehlern	a variety of plums

EATING OUT

Melone	mayloaner	melon (cantaloupe)
Nüsse	newsser	nuts
gemischte Nüsse	gehmishter newsser	assorted nuts
Pampelmuse	pahmperlmoozer	grapefruit
Pfirsich	pfeerzikh	peach
Pflaumen	pflowmern	plums
Preiselbeeren	prighzerlbayrern	cranberries
Quitte	kvitter	quince
Reineclauden	rainerkloadern	greengages
Rhabarber	rahbahrberr	rhubarb
Stachelbeeren	shtahkherlbayrern	gooseberries
Trauben	trowbern	grapes
Walnüsse	vahlnewsser	walnuts
Wassermelone	vahsserrmayloaner	watermelon
Weintrauben	vighntrowbern	grapes
Zuckermelone	tsukkerrmayloaner	honeydew melon
Zwetsch(g)en	tsvehtsh(g)ern	plums

Dessert

If you've survived all the courses on the menu, you may want
to say:

I'd like a dessert, please.	**Ich hätte gerne eine Nachspeise.**	ikh **hehter gehr**ner **igh**ner **nark**hshpighzer
Something light, please.	**Etwas Leichtes, bitte.**	**eht**vahss **lighkh**terss **bit**ter
Just a small portion.	**Nur eine kleine Portion.**	noor **igh**ner **kligh**ner portsyoan
Nothing more, thanks.	**Nein danke, nichts mehr.**	nighn **dahng**ker nikhtss mayr

If you aren't sure what to order, ask the waiter:

What do you recommend?	**Was empfehlen Sie?**	vahss ehmp**fay**lern zee

Here are some basic words you'll need to know if you want to
order a dessert:

-creme	-kraym	pudding
-eis, -glace	-ighss -glahsser	ice-cream
-kuchen	-kookhern	cake
-pudding	-pudding	pudding
-torte	-torter	layer cake

These flavours of ice-cream are popular throughout Germany:

Erdbeer-	ehrtbayr-	strawberry
Karamel-	kahrahmehl-	caramel
Mokka-	mokkah-	coffee
Schokoladen-	shokkollardern-	chocolate
Vanille-	vahniller-	vanilla
Zitronen-	tsitroanern-	lemon

Here are the names of some favourite biscuits (cookies):

Honigkuchen	hoanikhkookhern	honey biscuits
Leckerli	lehkerrli	gingersnaps
Makronen	mahkroanern	coconut macaroons
Printen	printern	honey biscuits
Spekulatius	shpehkoolartsiuss	almond biscuits

If you'd like to try something more filling with your coffee, we'd recommend...

Apfelstrudel (ahpferlshtrooderl)	paper-thin layers of pastry filled with apple slices, nuts, raisins and ham
Berliner (behrleenerr)	jam doughnut
Bienenstich (beenernshtikh)	honey-almond cake
Cremeschnitte (kraymshnitter)	napoleon
Gugelhupf (googerlhupf)	a moulded cake with a hole in the centre, usually filled with raisins and almonds
Hefekranz (hayferkrahnts)	ring-shaped coffee cake
Kaiserschmarren (kighzerrshmahrern)	shredded pancake with raisins served with syrup (Austrian)
Mohrenkopf (moarernkopf)	chocolate meringue with whipped-cream filling
Palatschinken (pahlahtshingkern)	pancakes, usually filled with jam, cheese, sausages or nuts and topped with hot chocolate sauce and nuts
Windbeutel (vintboyterl)	cream puff

The bill (check)

I'd like to pay.	Ich möchte gern zahlen.	ikh murkhter gehrn tsarlern
We'd like to pay separately.	Wir möchten getrennt bezahlen.	veer murkhtern gehtrehnt behtsarlern
You made a mistake in this bill, I think.	Ich glaube, Sie haben sich verrechnet.	ikh glowber zee harbern zikh ferrehkhnert
What is this amount for?	Wofür ist dieser Betrag?	voafewr ist deezerr behtrarg
Is service included?	Ist die Bedienung inbegriffen?	ist dee berdeenung inbergriffern
Do you accept traveller's cheques?	Kann ich mit Reise-schecks bezahlen?	kahn ikh mit righzershehks behtsarlern
Thank you, this is for you.	Danke, das ist für Sie.	dahngker dahss ist fewr zee
That was a very good meal.	Das Essen war sehr gut.	dahss ehssern varr zayr goot
We enjoyed it, thank you.	Danke, es hat gut geschmeckt.	dahngker ehss haht goot gehshmehkt

> **BEDIENUNG (NICHT) INBEGRIFFEN**
> SERVICE (NOT) INCLUDED

Complaints

But perhaps you'll have something to complain about:

That's not what I ordered. I asked for...	Das habe ich nicht bestellt. Ich wollte...	dahss harber ikh nikht behshtehlt. ikh volter
May I change this?	Können Sie mir dafür bitte etwas anderes bringen?	kurnern zee meer darfewr bitter ehtvahss ahnderrerss bringern
The meat is...	Das Fleisch ist...	dahss flighsh ist
overdone	zu stark gebraten	tsoo shtarrk gehbrartern
underdone (too rare)	zu roh	tsoo roa
too tough	zu zäh	tsoo tsai

EATING OUT

This is too...	Das ist zu ...	dahss ist tsoo
bitter/sour	bitter/sauer	bitterr/zowerr
salty/sweet	salzig/süß	zahltsikh/zewss
The food is cold.	Das Essen ist kalt.	dahss ehssern ist kahlt
What's taking you so long?	Weshalb dauert es so lange?	vehshahlp dowerrt ehss zoa lahnger
This isn't clean.	Das ist nicht sauber.	dahss ist nikht zowberr
Where are our drinks?	Wo bleiben unsere Getränke?	voa blighbern unzerrer gehtrehngker
Would you ask the head waiter to come over?	Würden Sie den Oberkellner zu uns bitten?	vewrdern zee dayn oaberrkehlnerr tsoo unss bittern

Drinks

Beer

Needless to say, beer is the national drink. Almost every town with a sizable population has at least one brewery. You'll want to try some of the local brews. However, Dortmund and Bavarian beer are found throughout the country.

I'd like a beer.	Ich hätte gern ein Bier.	ikh hehter gehrn ighn beer
I'd like a...of beer.	Ich hätte gern... Bier.	ikh hehter gehrn ... beer
a bottle	eine Flasche	ighner flahsher
a glass (1/2 pint)	ein Glas	ighn glarss
a large glass (a pint)	einen halben Liter	ighnern hahlbern leeterr
a mug (a quart)	eine Maß	ighner mars
Waiter! Another beer, please!	Herr Ober, noch ein Bier, bitte!	hehr oaberr nokh ighn beer bitter

Bier vom Faß (draught or draft beer) is considered to have a better taste and is less expensive, too, than bottled beer.

There are many different types of beer. You'll mainly have to ask for:

| a dark beer | ein Dunkles | ighn dungklerss |
| a light beer | ein Helles | ighn hehlerss |

But here are some other types of beer produced in German-speaking countries:

Altbier (ahltbeer)	a bitter beer with a high hops content
Bockbier, Doppelbock, Märzen, Starkbier (bokbeer, dopperlbok, mehrtsern, shtahrkbeer)	these are beers with a high alcoholic and malt content
Malzbier (mahltsbeer)	a dark, sweetish beer with a low alcoholic content but high in calories
Pilsener (pilzernerr)	has a particularly strong aroma of hops
Radlermaß (rardlerrmarss)	A light beer to which a bit of lemonade is added; in north Germany it's called *Alsterwasser* (**ahl**sterrvahsserr)
Weißbier (vighsbeer)	a light beer brewed from wheat grain; Berliners love a *Berliner Weiße mit Schuß—Weißbier* with a shot of raspberry juice.

Wine

The best wine-producing regions of Germany are those round the Rhine and Moselle rivers—the northernmost wine-producing areas of Europe.

More so than French vintners to the west, German wine producers are at the mercy of the vagaries of the country's climatic conditions. One type of wine can have a quite different character from one year to the next depending upon the weather. Therefore unless you're a German wine expert, you won't know from the wine list how the wine will taste.

For this reason, you'll have to learn to recognize a few basic terms on German labels which will tell you something about how you can likely expect a certain wine to taste. And the Germans are quite precise in labeling wine bottles.

In good years wine may be labeled *naturrein* or *Naturwein* which just means it's been produced under ordinary methods. In a bad year, sugar is sometimes added to increase the alcoholic content. If this is done, *verbessert* (improved) is euphemistically printed on the label.

The time-honoured rule of thumb on wine drinking has it that white wine goes well with fish, fowl and light meats while dark meats call for a red wine. A good rosé or dry sparkling wine goes well with almost anything and can accompany the whole meal. However, most German wine is white, and less attention is paid to the colour of wine.

There are four other words commonly found on German wine labels which you should know. They indicate the ripeness of the grapes when they were picked—or the degree of dryness or sweetness of the wine.

Spätlese (**spait**layzer)	gathered late after the normal harvesting; dry wine
Auslese (**ows**layzer)	selected gathering of particularly ripe bunches of grapes; slightly dry wine
Beerenauslese (**bay**rernowslayzer)	selected overripe grapes, slightly sweet wine
Trockenbeerenauslese (**trok**kernbayrern-owslayzer)	selected dried or raisin-like grapes; one drop of nectar can be squeezed out of each grape; a sweet or dessert wine is produced.

If none of these words appears on the label, you can assume that the wine results from a normal harvest and will therefore be fairly dry.

Don't miss the opportunity to sample local wine. Much of it doesn't travel well and is therefore rarely exported. The chart on the next page will help you to choose your wine.

In neighbouring German-speaking Switzerland, mostly red wine is produced. Austria's Wachau region along the fabled Danube riverbanks produces white wine while Burgenland to the east of Vienna has red wine.

If you need help in choosing a wine, don't hesitate to ask the waiter. He'll often suggest a bottle of local pride, perhaps a special bottling from the restaurateur's own wine cellar.

Type of wine	Examples	Accompanies
sweet white wine	Rheinpfalz is noted for wine in this category; bottles labeled *Trockenbeerenauslese* also fall into this section.	desserts, especially puddings and cake
dry white wine	The Rheingau region produces extraordinary white wine in good vintage years; Moselle wine can usually be counted on to be very dry; wine labelled *Spätlese* or *Auslese* can go into this category as well as those with the term *naturrein* or *Naturwein*.	cold meat or shellfish, fish, boiled meat, egg dishes, first courses, fowl, veal, dishes served with sauerkraut, sausages
rosé	Sometimes referred to as *Schillerwein*	goes with almost anything but especially cold dishes, eggs, pork, lamb
light-bodied red wine	Most local red wine fits into this category, particularly the wine of Austria's Burgenland, German-speaking Switzerland, the Ahr region (look for the names *Ahrweiler*, *Neuenahr* and *Walporzheim* on the label) and Baden-Württemberg.	roast chicken, turkey, veal, lamb, beef steak, ham, liver, quail, pheasant, stews, dishes served with gravy
full-bodied red wine	A difficult wine to find but a *Spätburgunder* from the Ahr Valley is a good example.	duck, goose, kidneys, most game, goulash, in short, any strong-flavoured preparations
sparkling wine	German *Sekt* comes into this category; some of it rivals French champagne in quality.	if it's dry, it goes with anything; may be drunk as an aperitif or as the climax to the dinner; goes well with shellfish, nuts and dried fruit; if it's sweet, it'll go nicely with dessert and pastry like *Strudel*

I'd like a... of...	Ich hätte gerne...	ikh hehter gehrner
bottle	eine Flasche	ighner flahsher
carafe	eine Karaffe	ighner kahrahfer
half bottle	eine halbe Flasche	ighner hahlber flahsher
litre	einen Liter	ighnern leeterr
1/2-pint glass	ein Viertel...	ighn feerterl
1/4-pint glass	ein Achtel...	ighn ahkhterl
I want a bottle of white/red wine.	Ich möchte eine Flasche Weißwein/ Rotwein.	ikh murkhter ighner flahsher vighsvighn/ roatvighn

If you enjoyed the wine, you may want to say:

Please bring me another...	Bitte bringen Sie mir noch...	bitter bringern zee mir nokh
Where does this wine come from?	Woher kommt dieser Wein?	voahayr komt deezerr vighn
What is the name of this wine?	Wie heißt dieser Wein?	vee highst deezerr vighn
How old is this wine?	Wie alt ist dieser Wein?	vee ahlt ist deezerr vighn

A refreshing highball for the ladies is sparkling wine and orange juice, *Damengedeck* (**dar**merngehdehk) or for the men, *Herrengedeck* (**heh**rerngehdehk), which is sparkling wine and beer.

dry	trocken	trokkern
full-bodied	vollmundig	volmundig
light	leicht	lighkht
red	rot	roat
rosé	rosé	roazay
sweet	süß	zewss
very dry	sehr trocken	zayr trokkern
white	weiß	vighss
chilled	gekühlt	gehkewlt
at room temperature	in Zimmertemperatur	in tsimmerr- tehmpayrahtoor

Other alcoholic drinks

Don't bother asking for any fancy cocktail or highball except in high-class restaurants.

aperitif	ein Aperitif	ighn ahpayritteef
beer	ein Bier	ighn beer
Bourbon	ein Bourbon	ighn "bourbon"
brandy	ein Weinbrand	ighn vighnbrahnt
cider	ein Apfelwein	ighn ahpferlvighn
cognac	ein Kognak	ighn konyahk
cordial	ein Likör	ighn likkurr
gin	ein Gin	ighn "gin"
gin-fizz	ein Gin-fizz	ighn "gin" fiss
gin and tonic	ein Gin mit Tonic	ighn "gin" mit tonnik
liqueur	ein Likör	ighn likkurr
mulled wine	ein Glühwein	ighn glewvighn
port	ein Portwein	ighn portvighn
rum	ein Rum	ighn rum
Scotch	ein Scotch	ighn "scotch"
sherry	ein Sherry	ighn "sherry"
vermouth	ein Wermut	ighn vayrmoot
vodka	ein Wodka	ighn votkah
whisky	ein Whisky	ighn "whisky"
and soda	mit Soda	mit soadah

glass	ein Glas	ighn glahss
bottle	eine Flasche	ighner flahsher
neat (straight)	pur	poor
on the rocks	mit Eis	mit ighss

You'll certainly want to take the occasion to sip a liqueur or brandy after your meal. The names of same well-known wine-distilled brandies are *Asbach-Uralt, Chantré* and *Dujardin.* Here are some other after-dinner drinks:

Apfelschnaps	ahpferlshnahpss	apple brandy
Aprikosenlikör	ahprikkoazernlikkurr	apricot liqueur
Birnenschnaps	beernernshnahpss	pear brandy
Bommerlunder	bommerrlunderr	caraway-flavoured brandy
Doornkaat	dornkart	German gin, juniper-berry brandy
Eierlikör	igherrlikkurr	eggflip, eggnog

EATING OUT

Heidelbeergeist	highderlbayrgighst	blueberry brandy
Himbeergeist	himbayrgighst	raspberry brandy
Himbeerlikör	himbayrlikurr	raspberry liqueur
Kirschlikör	kirshlikkurr	cherry liqueur
Kirschwasser	kirshvahsserr	cherry brandy
(Doppel)Korn	(dopperl)korn	grain-distilled liquor, akin to whisky
Kümmel	kewmerl	caraway-flavoured liquor
Obstler	oapstlerr	fruit brandy
Pflümli(wasser)	pflewmli(vahsserr)	plum brandy
Steinhäger	shtighnhaigerr	juniperberry brandy, akin to gin
Träsch	traish	pear and apple brandy
Weizenkorn	vightsernkorn	wheat-distilled liquor, akin to whisky
Zwetschgenwasser	tsvehtshgernvahsserr	plum brandy

I'd like a glass of..., please.	**Ich hätte gern ein Glas...**	ikh **heh**ter gehrn ighn glahss
Are there any local specialities?	**Haben Sie hiesige Spezialitäten?**	**har**bern zee **hee**zigger shpehtsiahlit**ai**tern
Please bring me a...	**Bitte bringen Sie mir einen...**	**bitter bring**ern zee mir **igh**nern

---

ZUM WOHL/PROST!
(tsum voal/proast)
CHEERS!

Other beverages

With coffee captured from the Turks after the siege of 1683, Europe's first café made its debut in Vienna. The *Kaffeehaus* (kah**fay**howss)—of which there are 800 today in the Austrian capital alone—is still an important institution where everyone from students and businessmen to housewives and artists can go to meet friends or associates, play cards, or read newspapers and periodicals. Though initiated in Vienna, the *Kaffeehaus* or *Café* takes on more or less the same importance throughout the rest of Austria as well as in Germany and Switzerland.

The ancient Arab dictum still reigns particularly in Viennese coffee shops: "Coffee must be as black as night, sweet as love and hot as hell." You can ask for anything in Austria from a *Nußschwarzer* (**nus**shvahrtserr) or *Neger* (**nay**gerr)—strong black coffee—to an *Einspänner* (**ighn**shpehnerr)—topped with whipped cream—or a *Melange* (may**lahng**zher)—coffee and hot milk topped with whipped cream. That whipped cream (called either *Schlag* or *Schlagobers*—shlarg, **shlarg**oaberrs in Austria) is the most important garnish for coffee and many pastries and can even be ordered as a side dish. *Kaffeehäuser* will serve anything from simple pastries to luscious, monumental sweet delicacies, and often snacks. Other types of coffee listed below are pretty much standard throughout German-speaking countries.

I'd like a/an...	Ich hätte gern...	ikh **hehter** gehrn
apple juice	einen Apfelsaft	**ighn**ern ahpferlzahft
(hot) chocolate	eine (heiße) Schokolade	**ighn**er (**highs**ser) shokkollarder
cup of coffee	eine Tasse Kaffee	**ighn**er tahsser kahfay
coffee	einen Kaffee	**ighn**ern kahfay
with cream	mit Sahne	mit **zar**ner
with milk	einen Milchkaffee	**ighn**ern milkhkahfay
black coffee	einen schwarzen Kaffee	**ighn**ern shvahrtsern kahfay
caffeine-free	einen koffein-freien Kaffee	**ighn**ern koffeheen-frighern kahfay
espresso coffee	einen Espresso	**ighn**ern ehsprehssoa
iced coffee	einen Eiskaffee	**ighn**ern ighskahfay
mokka	einen Mokka	**ighn**ern mokkah
(a glass of) milk	(ein Glas) Milch	(ighn) glahss milkh
milkshake	ein Milchmix-getränk	ighn milkhmiksgehtrehnk
mineral water	ein Mineralwasser	ighn minnehrarlvahsserr
orangeade	eine Orangeade	**ighn**er orahngzharder
sodawater	einen Sprudel	**ighn**ern shprooderl
squash (soda pop)	einen Fruchtsaft	**ighn**ern frukhtzahft
tea	einen Tee	**ighn**ern tay
with milk/lemon	mit Milch/mit Zitrone	mit milkh/mit tsi**troa**ner
iced tea	Eistee	**ighs**tay
peppermint tea	Pfefferminztee	pfehferr**mint**stay

Eating light—Snacks

The German *Schnellimbiß* (snack bar) offers a more limited choice of menu than we're used to at home. Since most of the snacks are on display, you won't need to say much more than:

I'll have one of those, please.	**Ich hätte gern eins von diesen.**	ikh hehter gehrn ighns fon deezern
Give me two of these and one of those.	**Geben Sie mir davon zwei und davon eins.**	gaybern zee meer darfon tsvigh unt darfon ighns
to the left / to the right	**links/rechts**	links/rehkhts
above / below	**darüber/darunter**	dahrewberr/dahrunterr
Please give me a / an / some...	**Bitte geben Sie mir...**	bitter gaybern zee meer
biscuits (Br.)	**Kekse**	kaykser
bread	**etwas Brot**	ehtvahss broat
butter	**etwas Butter**	ehtvahss butterr
cake	**Kuchen**	kookhern
candy	**etwas Konfekt**	ehtvahss konfehkt
chocolate bar	**eine Tafel Schokolade**	ighner tarferl shokkollarder
cookies	**Kekse**	kaykser
half a chicken	**ein halbes Hähnchen**	ighn hahlberss hainkhern
ice-cream	**ein Eis**	ighn ighss
pastry	**Gebäck**	gehbehk
roll	**ein Brötchen**	ighn brurtkhern
with cheese	**Käsebrötchen**	kaizerbrurtkhern
with fish	**Fischbrötchen**	fishbrurtkhern
with sausage	**Wurstbrötchen**	voorstbrurtkhern
salad	**Salat**	zahlart
sandwich	**ein Sandwich**	ighn sehndvitsh
toast	**etwas Toast**	ehtvahss toast
waffle	**eine Waffel**	ighner vahferl
How much is that?	**Was macht das?**	vahss mahkht dahss

Travelling around

Plane

Very brief—because at any airport or airline office you're sure to find someone who speaks English. But here are a few useful expressions you may want to know:

Is there a flight to Vienna?	**Gibt es einen Flug nach Wien?**	gipt ehss **igh**nern floog nahkh veen
Is it a nonstop flight?	**Ist es ein Direktflug?**	ist ehss ighn dee**rehkt**flug
When's the next plane to Hamburg?	**Wann geht die nächste Maschine nach Hamburg?**	vahn gayt dee **nehkh**ster mah**shee**ner nahkh **hahm**boorg
Do I have to change planes?	**Muß ich umsteigen?**	muss ikh **um**shtighern
Can I make a connection to Cologne?	**Kann ich einen Anschlußflug nach Köln buchen?**	kahn ikh **igh**nern **ahn**shlusfloog nahkh kurln **book**hern
I'd like a ticket to Zurich.	**Ich möchte einen Flug nach Zürich.**	ikh **murkh**ter **igh**nern floog nahkh **tse**wrikh
What's the fare to Berlin?	**Was kostet ein Flug nach Berlin?**	vahss **kos**tert ighn floog nahkh behr**leen**
single (one-way) return (roundtrip)	**einfacher Flug Rückflug**	**ighn**fahkherr floog **rewk**floog
What time does the plane take off?	**Wann startet die Maschine?**	vahn **shtahr**tert dee mah**shee**ner
What time do I have to check in?	**Wann muß ich mich melden?**	vahn muss ikh mikh **mehl**dern
What's the flight number?	**Welche Flugnummer ist es?**	**vehl**kher **floog**nummerr ist ehss
What time do we arrive?	**Wann landen wir?**	vahn **lahn**dern veer

ANKUNFT ARRIVAL	**ABFLUG** DEPARTURE

Train

If you're worried about railway tickets or time-tables, go to a travel agency where they speak English or see the desk-clerk at your hotel.

Travel on the main railway lines is generally fast, and the trains run on time. First-class coaches are comfortable; second-class, more than adequate.

To reach out-of-the-way places, you'll find frequent bus services available including the *Kraftpost* or *Postauto*.

Types of trains

TEE (tay ay ay)	Trans-Europ-Express: a luxury international service for which you pay a supplement. First class only, advance reservation required.
Expreß (ehks**prehss**)	A long-distance train, usually coming from or going abroad, stopping only at principal stations (Austria, Switzerland)
Fernschnellzug (fehrn**shnehl**tsoog)	Equivalent of the *Expreß* train (Germany).
Schnellzug (**shnehl**tsoog)	Long-distance train making a few more stops than an *Expreß* train (Austria, Switzerland)
D-Zug (**day**-tsoog)	Equivalent of the *Schnellzug* (Germany)
Städteschnellzug (**shteh**tershnehltsoog)	Long-distance train connecting principal cities and stopping only there (Switzerland)
Eilzug (**ighl**tsoog)	Medium-distance train, not stopping at small stations
Personenzug (**pehrzoa**nerntsoog)	Local train, stopping at all stations
Triebwagen (**treep**vargern)	Small diesel coach used for short runs
Schienenbus (**shee**nernbuss)	Equivalent of the *Triebwagen* (Germany)
Triebwagenschnellzug (**treep**vargernshnehltsoog)	Fast diesel used on long-distance runs (Austria)

Here are a few more useful terms:

Schlafwagen (**shlarf**vargern)	Sleeping-car with individual compartments (single, double, tourist) and toilet or lavatory facilities.
Liegewagen (**lee**gervargern)	A coach containing berths with blankets and pillows
Speisewagen (**shpigh**zervargern)	Dining-car
Gepäckwagen (**ger**pehkvargern)	Guard's van (baggage car) with only registered luggage permitted

To the railway station

Where's the railway station?	**Wo ist der Bahnhof?**	voa ist derr **barn**hoaf
Taxi, please!	**Taxi bitte!**	**tahk**si bitter
Take me to the railway station.	**Fahren Sie mich zum Bahnhof.**	**farr**ern zee mikh tsum **barn**hoaf
What's the fare?	**Wieviel macht es?**	vee**feel** mahkht ehss

EINGANG	ENTRANCE
AUSGANG	EXIT
ZU DEN BAHNSTEIGEN	TO THE PLATFORMS

Where's the...?

Where is / are the...?	**Wo ist/sind...?**	voa ist/zint
barber's	**der Herrenfriseur**	derr **heh**rernfrizurr
booking office	**die Platzreservierung**	dee **plahts**rehzerrveerung
buffet	**das Buffet**	dahss bew**fay**
currency-exchange office	**die Wechselstube**	dee **wehk**serlshtoober
information office	**die Auskunft**	dee **ows**kunft
restaurant	**das Restaurant**	dahss rehsto**rahng**
left-luggage office (baggage check)	**die Gepäckaufbewahrung**	dee ger**pehk**owfbervarrung
lost-property (lost and found) office	**das Fundbüro**	dahss **funt**bewroa

FOR TAXI, see page 27

luggage lockers	**die Schließfächer**	dee **shlees**fehkherr
news-stand	**der Zeitungsstand**	derr **tsight**ungsshtahnt
platform 7	**Bahnsteig 7**	**barn**shtighg 7
reservations office	**die Platz-reservierung**	dee **plahts**rehzerrveerung
ticket office	**der Fahrkarten-schalter**	derr **farr**kahrternshahlterr
waiting-room	**der Wartesaal**	derr **vahr**terzarl
Where are the toilets ?	**Wo sind die Toiletten ?**	voa zint dee toah**leh**tern

Inquiries

When is the...train to Kiel ?	**Wann geht der... Zug nach Kiel ?**	vahn gayt derr... tsoog nahkh keel
first/last/next	**erste/letzte/nächste**	**ehr**ster/**leht**ster/**neh**..ster
What time does the train for Karlsruhe leave ?	**Wann fährt der Zug nach Karlsruhe ?**	vahn fairt derr tsoog nahkh **karrls**rooer
What's the fare to Basle ?	**Was kostet die Fahrt nach Basel ?**	vahss **kos**tert dee farrt nahkh **bar**zerl
Is it a through train ?	**Ist es ein durch-gehender Zug ?**	ist ehss ighn **doorkh**gayernderr tsoog
What time does the train arrive at Münster ?	**Wann kommt der Zug in Münster an ?**	vahn komt derr tsoog in **mewn**sterr ahn
Is there a dining-car on the train ?	**Hat der Zug einen Speisewagen ?**	haht derr tsoog **igh**nern **shpigh**zervargern
Is there a sleeping-car on the train ?	**Hat der Zug einen Schlafwagen ?**	haht derr tsoog **igh**nern **shlarf**vargern
Does the train stop at Ingolstadt ?	**Hält der Zug in Ingolstadt ?**	hehlt derr tsoog in **ingol**shtaht
What platform does the train for Bonn leave from ?	**Auf welchem Gleis fährt der Zug nach Bonn ab ?**	owf **vehl**kherm glighss fairt derr tsoog nahkh bon ahp
What platform does the train from Hamburg arrive at ?	**Auf welchem Gleis kommt der Zug aus Hamburg an ?**	owf **vehl**kherm glighss komt derr tsoog owss **ham**boorg ahn
I'd like to buy a time-table.	**Ich hätte gerne einen Fahrplan.**	ikh **heh**ter gehrn **igh**nern **farr**plarn

Es ist ein durchgehender Zug.	It's a through train.
Sie müssen in ... umsteigen.	You have to change at...
Steigen Sie in Heidelberg in einen Personenzug um.	Change at Heidelberg and get a local train.
Bahnsteig 7 ist...	Platform 7 is...
dort drüben/oben links/rechts	over there/upstairs on the left/on the right
Es gibt einen Zug nach Bonn um...	There's a train to Bonn at...
Ihr Zug fährt auf Bahnsteig ... ab.	Your train will leave from platform...
Der Zug hat... Minuten Verspätung.	There'll be a delay of... minutes.

Tickets

I want a ticket to Stuttgart.	Ich möchte eine Fahrkarte nach Stuttgart.	ikh murkhter ighner farr-kahrter nahkh shtutgahrt
single (one-way)	eine einfache Fahrkarte	ighner ighnfahkher farrkahrter
return (roundtrip)	eine Rückfahrkarte	ighner rewkfarrkahrter
first class	erste Klasse	ehrster klahsser
second class	zweite Klasse	tsvighter klahsser
Isn't it half price for the boy/girl?	Kann der Junge/das Mädchen zum halben Preis fahren?	kahn derr yunger/dahss maitkhern tsoom hahlbern prighss farrern
He's/She's 13.	Er/Sie ist 13.	ehr/zee ist 13

Erste oder zweite Klasse?	First or second class?
Einfache oder Rückfahrt-karte?	Single or return (one-way or roundtrip)?
Wie alt ist er/sie?	How old is he/she?

All aboard...

Is this the right platform for the train to Vienna?	**Ist das der richtige Bahnsteig für den Zug nach Wien?**	ist dahss derr **rik**htigger **barn**shtighg fewr dayn tsoog nahkh veen
Is this the right train to Graz?	**Ist das der Zug nach Graz?**	ist dahss derr tsoog nahkh grarts
Excuse me. May I get by?	**Verzeihung. Darf ich bitte durchgehen?**	fehrtsighung. dahrf ikh **bitter doorkh**gayern
Is this seat taken?	**Ist dieser Platz besetzt?**	ist **dee**zerr plahts ber**zeht**st
I think that's my seat.	**Ich glaube, das ist mein Platz.**	ikh **glow**ber dahss ist mighn plahts
Would you let me know before we get to Bamberg?	**Könnten Sie mir Bescheid geben, wenn wir in Bamberg ankommen?**	**kurn**ten zee meer ber**shight gay**bern vehn veer in **bahm**behrg **ahn**kommern
What station is this?	**Wie heißt dieser Ort?**	vee highst **dee**zerr ort
How long does the train stop here?	**Wie lange hält der Zug hier?**	vee **lahng**er hehlt derr tsoog heer
When do we get to Cologne?	**Wann kommen wir in Köln an?**	vahn **kom**mern veer in kurln ahn

Sometime on the journey the ticket-collector (*der Schaffner*—derr **shahf**nerr) will come around and say: *Fahrkarten, bitte* (Tickets, please)!

Eating

If you want a full meal in the dining-car, you may have to get a ticket from the attendant who'll come to your compartment. There are usually two sittings for lunch and dinner.

You can get snacks and drinks in the buffet-car and in the dining-car when it isn't being used for main meals. On some trains an attendant comes around with a cart with snacks, tea, coffee and soft drinks. At the larger stations an attendant with a refreshment wagon walks alongside the train and takes orders through the window.

| First/Second call for dinner. | **Erster/Zweiter Aufruf zum Essen.** | ehrsterr/**tsvigh**terr **ow**froof tsum **ehss**ern |
| Where's the dining-car? | **Wo ist der Speisewagen?** | voa ist derr **shpigh**zer-vargern |

Sleeping

Are there any free compartments in the sleeping-car?	**Sind noch Abteile im Schlafwagen frei?**	zint nokh ahp**tigh**ler im **shlarf**vargern frigh
Where's the sleeping-car?	**Wo ist der Schlafwagen?**	voa ist derr **shlarf**vargern
Where's my berth?	**Wo ist mein Bett?**	voa ist mighn beht
Compartments 18 and 19 please.	**Abteile 18 und 19, bitte.**	ahp**tigh**ler 18 unt 19 **bit**ter
I'd like a lower berth.	**Ich möchte eine untere Liege.**	ikh **murkh**ter **igh**ner **un**terrer **lee**ger
Would you make up our berths?	**Würden Sie unsere Betten machen?**	**vewr**dern zee **un**zerrer **beh**tern **mah**khern
Would you call me at 7 o'clock?	**Würden Sie mich um 7 Uhr wecken?**	**vewr**dern zee mikh um 7 oor **veh**kern
Would you bring me coffee in the morning?	**Würden Sie mir bitte in der Frühe Kaffee bringen?**	**vewr**dern zee meer **bit**ter in der **frew**er **kah**fay **bring**ern

Baggage and porters

| Porter! | **Gepäckträger!** | ger**pehk**traigerr |
| Can you help me with my bags? | **Können Sie mir mit meinem Gepäck helfen?** | **kur**nern zee meer mit **migh**nerm ger**pehk** **hehl**fern |

Note: If you want to put your luggage in the guard's van (baggage car), be sure to have it insured.

| Can I insure these bags? | **Kann ich dieses Gepäck versichern?** | kahn ikh **dee**zers ger**pehk** fehr**zee**kherrn |

FOR PORTERS, see also page 24

Lost!

We hope you'll have no need for the following phrases on your trip... but just in case:

Where's the lost-property (lost-and-found) office?	**Wo ist das Fundbüro?**	voa ist dahss **funt**bewroa
I've lost...	**Ich habe...verloren.**	ikh harber...fehrloarern
this morning	**heute morgen**	hoyter morgern
yesterday	**gestern**	gehsterrn
I lost it in...	**Ich habe es in... verloren.**	ikh harber ehss in... fehrloarern
It's very valuable.	**Es ist sehr wertvoll.**	ehss ist zayr **vayrt**fol

Underground (subway)

The *U-Bahn* (**oo**-barn) in Hamburg, Berlin, Frankfurt and Munich corresponds to the London underground or the New York subway. Lines extend from the centre of the city to the suburbs. A map showing the various lines and stations is displayed outside every station. Pocket maps can be obtained from news-stands and travel agents. Some *U-Bahnen* are still under construction.

The fare is always the same, irrespective of the distance you travel. If you intend to use the *U-Bahn* regularly, get a book of tickets (*ein Fahrscheinheft*—ighn **farr**shighnhehft). This will mean a small saving on fares.

The *U-Bahn* is closed from 1 to 5 a.m.

Where's the nearest underground station?	**Wo ist die nächste U-Bahnstation?**	voa ist dee **nehkh**ster oo-barnshtahtsioan
Does this train go to...?	**Fährt dieser Zug nach...?**	fairt **dee**zerr tsoog nahkh
Where do I change for...?	**Wo muß ich nach... umsteigen?**	voa muss ikh nahkh... umshtighgern
Is the next station...?	**Ist die nächste Station...?**	ist dee **nehkh**ster shtahtsioan

Bus—Tram (streetcar)

In most cities you'll find automatic ticket dispensers at each stop enabling you to buy your ticket in advance. In some rural buses, you may find the driver also acting as conductor. In big cities you can buy a booklet of tickets for regular journeys.

I'd like a booklet of tickets.	**Ich möchte ein Fahrscheinheft.**	ikh **murkh**ter ighn farr**shighn**hehft
Which tram (streetcar) goes to the centre of town?	**Welche Straßenbahn fährt ins Stadt-zentrum?**	vehlkher shtrahssern-barn fairt ins **shtaht**-tsehntrum
Where can I get a bus into town?	**Wo hält der Bus, der ins Stadt-zentrum fährt?**	voa hehlt derr buss derr ins **shtaht**-tsehntrum fairt
What bus do I take for...?	**Welchen Bus muß ich nach... nehmen?**	vehlkhern buss muss ikh nahkh...**nay**mern
Where's the...?	**Wo ist...?**	voa ist
bus stop	**die Bushaltestelle**	dee **buss**hahltershtehler
terminus	**die Endstation**	dee **ehnt**shtahtsioan
When is the...bus to Sankt Pauli?	**Wann fährt der... Bus nach Sankt Pauli?**	vahn fairt derr...buss nahkh sahnkt **pow**lee
first / last / next	**erste/letzte/nächste**	**ehr**ster / **leht**ster / **nehkh**ster
How often do the buses to the airport run?	**Wie oft fahren die Busse zum Flughafen?**	vee oft **far**rern dee **buss**er tsum **floog**harfern
How much is the fare to...?	**Was kostet es nach...?**	vahss **kost**ert ehss nahkh
Do I have to change buses?	**Muß ich umsteigen?**	muss ikh **um**shtighgern
How long does the journey take?	**Wie lange dauert die Fahrt?**	vee **lahng**er **dow**errt dee fahrt

BUSHALTESTELLE	REGULAR BUS STOP
BEDARFSHALTESTELLE	STOPS ON REQUEST

| Will you tell me when to get off? | **Können Sie mir bitte sagen, wann ich aussteigen muß?** | kurnern zee meer bitter zargern vahn ikh owsshtighgern muss |
| Please let me off at the next stop. | **Lassen Sie mich bitte an der nächsten Haltestelle aussteigen.** | lahssern zee mikh bitter ahn derr nehkhstern hahlter- shtehler owsshtighgern |

Boats

River boats ply up and down the Rhine and Mosel rivers. A boat trip on the Bonn-Rüdesheim stretch of the Rhine, with its medieval castles and steep vineyards, is well worthwhile.

There's also a river-boat connection from Basle, Switzerland, all the way down to Rotterdam in the Netherlands.

There's regular boat service on the River Danube with some steamers offering cabins for overnight trips. The line begins at Passau, West Germany, continues through the wine-producing region of the Wachau and ends in Vienna. But you can follow the Danube to the east from Vienna via Budapest, for instance.

Other modes of transportation

You may also want to try one of these to get around:

bicycle	**das Fahrrad**	dahss farrrart
boat	**das Boot**	dahss boat
motorboat	**das Motorboot**	dahss moatorboat
rowing-boat	**das Ruderboot**	dahss rooderrboat
sailing-boat	**das Segelboot**	dahss zaygerlboat
helicopter	**der Hubschrauber**	derr hoopshrowberr
hitch-hiking	**trampen**	trahmpern
horseback riding	**reiten**	rightern
hovercraft	**das Luftkissenboot**	dahss luftkissernboat
moped (motor-bike)	**das Motorrad**	dahss moatorrart
motorcycle	**das Moped**	dahss moapeht

And if you're really stuck, go...

| walking | **zu Fuß gehen** | tsu fooss gayern |

TRAVELLING AROUND

Around and about—Sightseeing

Here we're more concerned with the cultural aspect of life than with entertainment and, for the moment, with towns rather than the countryside. If you want a guide book, ask...

Can you recommend a good guide book for...?	**Können Sie einen guten Reiseführer über...empfehlen?**	kurnern zee ighnern gootern righzerfewrerr ewberr ... ehmpfaylern
Is there a tourist office?	**Gibt es ein Fremdenverkehrsbüro?**	gipt ehss ighn frehmdernfehrkayrsbewroa
Where's the tourist office?	**Wo ist das Fremdenverkehrsbüro?**	voa ist dahss frehmdernfehrkayrsbewroa
What are the main points of interest?	**Was sind die Hauptsehenswürdigkeiten?**	vahss zint dee howptzayernsvewrdikhkightern
We're here for...	**Wir sind für...hier.**	veer zint fewr...heer
a few hours	**ein paar Stunden**	ighn parr shtundern
a day	**einen Tag**	ighnern targ
three days	**drei Tage**	drigh targer
a week	**eine Woche**	ighner vokher
Can you recommend a sightseeing tour?	**Können Sie eine Stadtrundfahrt empfehlen?**	kurnern zee ighner shtahtruntfarrt ehmpfaylern
Where does the bus start from?	**Wo fährt der Bus ab?**	voa fairt derr buss ahp
Will it pick us up at the hotel?	**Holt er uns im Hotel ab?**	hoalt ehr uns im hotehl ahp
How much does the tour cost?	**Was kostet die Rundfahrt?**	vahss kostert dee runtfarrt
What time does the tour start?	**Wann beginnt die Rundfahrt?**	vahn bergint dee runtfarrt
What bus/What tram (streetcar) do we take?	**Welchen Bus/ Welche Straßenbahn müssen wir nehmen?**	vehlkhern buss/vehlkher shtrarssernbarn mewssern veer naymern
We'd like to rent a car for the day.	**Wir möchten gern für heute einen Wagen mieten.**	veer murkhtern gehrn fewr hoyter ighnern vargern meetern

FOR TIME OF DAY, see page 178

SIGHTSEEING

Is there an English-speaking guide?	**Gibt es einen englischsprechenden Fremdenführer?**	gipts ehss **ighnern** ehnglishshprehkherndern frehmdernfewrerr
Where is/Where are the...?	**Wo ist/Wo sind...?**	voa ist/voa zint
abbey	**das Kloster**	dahss **kloasterr**
amusement park	**der Vergnügungspark**	derr fehrgnewgungspahrk
aquarium	**das Aquarium**	dahss **ahkvarrium**
artists' quarter	**das Künstlerviertel**	dahss **kewnstlerfeerterl**
botanical gardens	**der Botanische Garten**	derr bottarnisher **gahrtern**
building	**das Gebäude**	dahss gerboyder
business district	**das Geschäftsviertel**	dahss gershehftsfeertel
castle	**das Schloß/die Burg**	dahss shloss/dee boorg
catacombs	**die Katakomben**	dee kahtah**kombern**
cathedral	**die Kathedrale/der Dom**	dee kahtehdrarler/derr doam
cave	**die Höhle**	dee hurler
cemetery	**der Friedhof**	derr **freethoaf**
circus	**der Zirkus**	derr tseerkuss
city centre	**die Stadtmitte**	dee shtahtmitter
city hall	**das Rathaus**	dahss rarthowss
city walls	**die Stadtmauern**	dee shtahtmowerr
church	**die Kirche**	dee keerkher
concert hall	**die Konzerthalle**	dee kontsehrthahler
convent	**das Nonnenkloster**	dahss nonnernkloasterr
convention hall	**die Kongreßhalle**	dee kongrehshahler
court house	**das Gericht**	dahss gerrikht
docks	**die Hafenanlagen**	dee harfernahnlargern
downtown area	**die Innenstadt**	dee innernshtaht
exhibition	**die Ausstellung**	dee owsshtehlung
factory	**die Fabrik**	dee fahbrik
fortress	**die Festung**	dee fehstung
fountain	**der Brunnen/Springbrunnen**	derr brunnern/shpringbrunnern
gallery	**die Galerie**	dee gahlehree
gardens	**die Grünanlagen**	dee grewnahnlargern
government building	**das Regierungsgebäude**	dahss rehgeerungsgerboyder
harbour	**der Hafen**	derr harfern
lake	**der See**	derr zay
library	**die Bibliothek**	dee biblioatayk
market	**der Markt**	derr mahrkt
memorial	**das Denkmal**	dahss **dehngk**marl
monastery	**das Kloster**	dahss kloasterr
monument	**das Denkmal**	dahss **dehngk**marl

FOR ASKING THE WAY, see also page 144

museum	das Museum	dahss muzayum
observatory	das Observatorium	dahss opzehrvahtoarium
old city	die Altstadt	dee ahltshtaht
opera house	das Opernhaus	dahss oaperrnhowss
palace	der Palast/das Schloß	derr pahlahst/dahss shloss
park	der Park	derr pahrk
parliament building	das Parlaments-gebäude	dahss pahrlahmehnts-gerboyder
river	der Fluß	derr fluss
ruins	die Ruinen	dee rueenern
shopping centre	das Einkaufszentrum	dahss ighnkowfstsehntrum
stadium	das Stadion	dahss shtardion
statue	die Statue	dee shtartuer
stock exchange	die Börse	dee burrzer
television studio	das Fernsehstudio	dahss fehrnzayshtoodio
theatre	das Theater	dahss tayarterr
tomb	die Gruft	dee gruft
tower	der Turm	derr toorm
university	die Universität	dee unnivehrzitayt
zoo	der Zoo	derr tsoa

Admission

Is... open on Sundays?	Ist...sonntags geöffnet?	ist...zontargs gerurfnert
When does it open?	Wann wird geöffnet?	vahn veert gerurfnert
When does it close?	Wann schließt es?	vahn shleest ehss
How much is the entrance fee?	Was kostet der Eintritt?	vahss kostert derr ighntrit
Is there any reduction for...?	Gibt es Ermäßigung für...?	gipt ehss ehrmaissigung fewr
students / children	Studenten/Kinder	shtuddehntern / kinderr
Have you a guidebook (in English)?	Haben Sie einen Führer (in Englisch)?	harbern zee ighnern fewrerr (in ehnglish)
Is it all right to take pictures?	Darf man photographieren?	dahrf mahn fottograhfeerern

| EINTRITT FREI | ADMISSION FREE |
| PHOTOGRAPHIEREN VERBOTEN | NO CAMERAS ALLOWED |

SIGHTSEEING

Who—What—When?

What's that building?	Was für ein Gebäude ist das?	vahss fewr ighn gerboyder ist dahss
Who was the...?	Wer war der...?	vayr varr derr
architect	Architekt	ahrkhittehkt
artist	Künstler	kewnstlerr
painter	Maler	marlerr
sculptor	Bildhauer	bilthowerr
Who built it?	Wer hat es gebaut?	vayr haht ehss gerbowt
Who painted that picture?	Wer hat das Bild gemalt?	vayr haht dahss bilt germarlt
When did he live?	Wann hat er gelebt?	vahn haht ehr gerlaybt
When was it built?	Wann wurde es erbaut?	vahn woorder ehss ehrbowt
Where's the house where...lived?	Wo ist das Haus, in dem...wohnte?	voa ist dahss howss in daym...voanter
We're interested in...	Wir interessieren uns für...	veer intehrehsseerern uns fewr
antiques	Antiquitäten	ahntikvittaytern
archaeology	Archäologie	ahrkhehoaloagee
art	Kunst	kunst
botany	Botanik	bottarnik
ceramics	Keramik	kehrarmik
coins	Münzen	mewntsern
crafts	Handwerk	hahntvehrk
fine arts	bildende Künste	bildernder kewnster
furniture	Möbel	murberl
geology	Geologie	gayoaloagee
history	Geschichte	gershikhter
medicine	Medizin	mehditseen
music	Musik	muzeek
natural history	Naturkunde	nahtoorkunder
ornithology	Vogelkunde	foagerlkunder
painting	Malerei	marlehrigh
pottery	Töpferei	turpfehrigh
prehistory	Urgeschichte	oorgershikhter
sculpture	Bildhauerei	bilthowerrigh
zoology	Zoologie	tsoaoaloagee
Where's the...department?	Wo ist die ...abteilung?	voa ist dee...ahptighlung

Just the adjective you've been looking for...

It's...	Es ist...	ehss ist
amazing	erstaunlich	ehrshtownlikh
awful	scheußlich	shoysslikh
beautiful	schön	shurn
gloomy	düster	dewsterr
impressive	eindrucksvoll	ighndruksfol
interesting	interessant	intehrehssahnt
magnificent	herrlich	hehrlikh
monumental	großartig	groassahrtikh
overwhelming	überwältigend	ewberrvehltiggernt
sinister	unheimlich	unhighmlikh
strange	seltsam	zehltzahm
superb	hervorragend	hehrfoarrargernt
terrible	schrecklich	shrehklikh
terrifying	entsetzlich	ehntzehtslikh
tremendous	außerordentlich	owsserrorderntlikh
ugly	häßlich	hehsslikh

Religious services

Most churches and cathedrals are open to the public except, of course, when a service is being conducted.

If you're interested in taking photographs, you should obtain permission first.

Services are conducted in English in many towns. Ask the local tourist office for further details.

Is there a... church near here?	Gibt es eine... Kirche in der Nähe?	gipt ehss ighner... keerkher in derr neher
Catholic	katholische	kahtoalisher
Protestant	evangelische	ehvahngaylisher
At what time is...?	Wann beginnt...?	vahn bergint
mass	die Messe	dee mehsser
the service	der Gottesdienst	derr gottersdeenst
Where can I find a...who speaks English?	Wo finde ich einen..., der Englisch spricht?	voa finder ikh ighnern... derr ehnglish shprikht
priest/minister	Priester/Pfarrer	preesterr/pfahrerr

Relaxing

Cinema (movies)—Theatre

Foreign films are usually dubbed into German, though some
cinemas also screen them in the original, with German
subtitles, at certain times on certain days. Since cinema
showings are seldom continuous you can buy your tickets in
advance.

Theatre curtain time is about 8 p.m. Advance booking is
advisable.

You can find out what's playing from newspapers and bill-
boards. In most large towns you can buy a publication of
the type "This Week in...".

Have you a copy of "This Week in..."?	**Haben Sie einen «Veranstaltungskalender von...»?**	harbern zee ighnern fehrahnshtahltungskahlehn derr fon
What's showing at the cinema tonight?	**Was gibt es heute abend im Kino zu sehen?**	vahss gipt ehss hoyter arbernt im keenoa tsu zayern
What's playing at the...theatre?	**Was wird im ...theater gegeben?**	vahss veert im ...tayarterr gergaybern
What sort of play is it?	**Was für ein Stück ist es?**	vahss fewr ighn shtewk ist ehss
Who's it by?	**Von wem ist es?**	fon vaym ist ehss
Can you recommend (a)...?	**Können Sie mir ...empfehlen?**	kurnern zee meer ...ehmpfaylern
good film	**einen guten Film**	ighnern gootern film
comedy	**eine Komödie**	ighner kommurdier
something light	**etwas Leichtes**	ehtvahss lighkhters
drama	**ein Drama**	ighn drarmar
musical	**ein Musical**	ighn "musical"
revue	**eine Revue**	ighner rehvew
thriller	**einen Krimi**	ighnern krimmi
Western	**einen Western**	ighnern vehstern
At what theatre is that new play by...being performed?	**In welchem Theater wird das neue Stück von...gespielt?**	in vehlkherm tayarterr veert dahss noyer shtewk fon...gershpeelt

Where's that new film by…being shown?	**Wo läuft der neue Film von…?**	voa loyft derr **noyer** film fon
Who's in it?	**Wer spielt mit?**	vayr shpeelt mit
Who's the director?	**Wer ist der Regisseur?**	vayr it derr rehzhi**ssurr**
What time does the show begin?	**Wann beginnt die Vorstellung?**	vahn ber**gint** dee **foar**shtehlung
What time does the show end?	**Wann ist die Vorstellung zu Ende?**	vahn ist dee **foar**shtehlung tsu **ehn**der
What time does the first evening performance start?	**Um wieviel Uhr beginnt die erste Abendvorstellung?**	um **vee**feel oor ber**gint** dee **ehr**ster **arbernt**foarshtehlung
Are there any tickets for tonight?	**Gibt es noch Karten für heute abend?**	gipt ehss nokh **kahr**tern fewr **hoy**ter **arbernt**
How much are the tickets?	**Wie teuer sind die Karten?**	vee **toyerr** zint dee **kahr**tern
I want to reserve 2 tickets for the show on Friday evening.	**Ich möchte 2 Karten für Freitag abend vorbestellen.**	ikh **murkht**er 2 **kahr**tern fewr **frightarg arbernt foar**bershtehlern
Can I have a ticket for the matinée on Tuesday?	**Kann ich eine Karte für die Nachmittagsvorstellung am Dienstag bekommen?**	kahn ikh **ighn**er **kahr**ter fewr dee **nahkh**mittahgs-foarshtehlung ahm **deen**starg berkommern
I want a seat in the stalls (orchestra).	**Ich hätte gern einen Platz im Parkett.**	ikh **hehter gehrn ighnern plahts** im pahr**keht**
Not too far back.	**Nicht zu weit hinten.**	nikht tsu vight **hintern**
Somewhere in the middle.	**Irgendwo in der Mitte.**	**eer**gerntvoa in derr **mitter**
How much are the seats in the circle (mezzanine)?	**Wie teuer sind die Plätze im ersten Rang?**	vee **toyer** zint dee **plehtser** im **ehrstern** rahng
May I please have a programme?	**Kann ich bitte ein Programm haben?**	kahn ikh **bitter** ighn pro**grahm** harbern
Can I check this coat?	**Kann ich den Mantel abgeben?**	kahn ikh dayn **mahnterl** ahp**gaybern**

Bedaure, es ist alles ausverkauft.	I'm sorry, we're sold out.
Es gibt nur noch ein paar Plätze im ersten Rang.	There are only a few seats left in the circle (mezzanine).
Darf ich Ihre Eintrittskarte sehen?	May I see your ticket?
Hier ist Ihr Platz.	This is your seat.

Opera—Ballet—Concert

Where's the opera house?	**Wo ist das Opernhaus?**	voa ist dahss oaperrnhowss
Is there an operetta playing this evening?	**Wird heute abend eine Operette gespielt?**	veert hoyter arbernt ighner oaperrehtter gershpeelt
Where's the concert hall?	**Wo ist die Konzerthalle?**	voa ist dee kontsehrthaler
What's on at the opera tonight?	**Was wird heute abend in der Oper gegeben?**	vahss veert hoyter arbernt in derr oaperr gergaybern
Who's singing?	**Wer singt?**	vayr zingt
Who's dancing?	**Wer tanzt?**	vayr tahntst
What time does the programme start?	**Wann beginnt die Vorstellung?**	vahn bergint dee foarshtehlung
What orchestra is playing?	**Welches Orchester spielt?**	vehlkhers orkehsterr shpeelt
What are they playing?	**Was wird gespielt?**	vahss veert gershpeelt
Who's the conductor?	**Wer ist der Dirigent?**	vayr ist derr dirrigehnt

RELAXING

Night-clubs

There are top night-clubs in major cities which are somewhat expensive. Find out the prices before you order—and allow for the various surcharges.

Night-time entertainment, however, is generally less showy, more intimate in Germany, Austria and Switzerland. Even in provincial towns you'll find a *Heuriger* (**hoy**rigerr), *Bierhalle* (**beer**hahler), *Bier-* or *Weinstube* (**vighn**shtoober) where a small band or orchestra may play light music from drinking songs to operatic airs. A costumed chorus often sings and encourages the customers to join in. Such a night spot is very popular and informal, a good place to meet the locals and inexpensive.

Can you recommend a good night-club?	**Können Sie ein gutes Nachtlokal empfehlen?**	kurnern zee ighn gooterss nahkhtlokkarl ehmpfaylern
Is there a floor show?	**Gibt es Attraktionen?**	gipt ehss ahtrahktsioanern
What time does the floor show start?	**Wann beginnt das Programm?**	vahn bergint dahss programh
Is evening dress necessary?	**Wird Abendgarde- robe verlangt?**	veert arberntgahrdehroaber fehrlahngt

And once inside...

A table for 2, please.	**Einen Tisch für 2, bitte.**	ighnern tish fewr 2 bitter
My name's...I reserved a table for 4.	**Ich heiße...Ich habe einen Tisch für 4 Personen reservieren lassen.**	ikh highsser..ikh harber ighnern tish fewr 4 pehrzoanern rehzerrveerern lahssern
I telephoned you earlier.	**Ich habe vor einer Weile angerufen.**	ikh harber foar ighnerr vighler ahngerroofern
We haven't got a reservation.	**Wir haben nicht reservieren lassen.**	veer harbern nikht rehzerrveerern lahssern

RELAXING

Dancing

Where can we go dancing?	**Wohin können wir tanzen gehen?**	voahin kurnern veer tahntsern gayern
Is there a discotheque in town?	**Gibt es hier eine Diskothek?**	gipt ehss heer **ighner** diskoathayk
There's a dance at the...	**Im...findet ein Ball statt.**	im...findert ighn bahl shtaht
Would you like to dance?	**Darf ich bitten?**	dahrf ikh bittern
May I have this dance?	**Darf ich um diesen Tanz bitten?**	dahrf ikh um **deezern** tahnts bittern

Do you happen to play...?

On a rainy day, this page may solve your problems.

Do you happen to play chess?	**Spielen Sie etwa Schach?**	shpeelern zee ehtvar shahkh
I'm afraid I don't.	**Leider nein.**	**ligh**derr nighn
No, but I'll give you a game of draughts (checkers).	**Nein, aber ich spiele mit Ihnen Dame.**	nighn arberr ikh shpeeler mit eenern darmer
king	**der König**	derr kurnikh
queen	**die Dame**	dee darmer
castle (rook)	**der Turm**	derr toorm
bishop	**der Läufer**	derr loyferr
knight	**der Springer**	derr shpringerr
pawn	**der Bauer**	derr bowerr
Checkmate!	**Schachmatt!**	shahkhmaht
Do you play cards?	**Spielen Sie Karten?**	shpeelern zee kahrtern
bridge	**Bridge**	"bridge"
gin rummy	**Rommé**	rommay
whist	**Whist**	"whist"
pontoon (21)	**Siebzehn und Vier**	zeebtsayn unt feer
poker	**Poker**	poakerr
hearts	**Herz**	kehrts
diamonds	**Karo**	karroa
clubs	**Kreuz**	kroyts
spades	**Pik**	hehrts

RELAXING

ace	**das As**	dahss ahss
king	**der König**	derr kurnikh
queen	**die Dame**	dee darmer
jack	**der Bube**	derr boober
joker	**der Joker**	derr joakerr

Casino

You'll find casinos at most resorts and spas in Germany, Austria and Switzerland. Most stay open all year round but the usual season runs from Easter until mid-October.

Boule—similar to roulette—is the only game played in the modest casinos of Switzerland.

To get into a casino, you'll need your passport. You must be over 21. You must also have a "clean record" in the gambling world. As far as you're concerned, you need have no doubts about the honesty of the game. All legitimate casinos· are strictly controlled and regularly inspected. Casinos are anxious to avoid any risk of scandal or adverse public relations.

Entrance fees are nominal. The language of the casino is mostly German but the croupiers will understand enough English (or French) for your requirements.

For those who like to bet on horses there are a number of race courses. More modest gamblers can take advantage of some of the state-run football pools and lotteries.

RELAXING

FOR NUMBERS, see page 175

Sports

You name the sport, and you'll doubtless be able to find it in Germany, Austria and Switzerland. The most popular spectator sport is by far football (soccer).

Where's the nearest golf course?	**Wo ist der nächste Golfplatz?**	voa ist derr nehkhster golfplahts
Can we hire (rent) clubs?	**Können wir Golfschläger leihen?**	kurnern veer golfshlaigerr lighern
Where are the tennis courts?	**Wo sind die Tennisplätze?**	voa zint dee tehnisplehtser
Can I hire rackets?	**Kann ich Tennis- schläger leihen?**	kahn ikh tehnisshlaigerr lighern
What's the charge per...?	**Wieviel kostet es pro...?**	veefeel kostert ehss proa
day/round/hour	**Tag/Runde/Stunde**	targ/runder/shtunder
Where's the nearest race course (track)?	**Wo ist die nächste Pferderennbahn?**	voa ist dee nehkhster pfehrderrehnbarn
What's the admission charge?	**Was kostet der Eintritt?**	vahss kostert derr ighntrit
Is there a swimming pool here?	**Gibt es hier ein Schwimmbad?**	gipt ehss heer ighn shvimbart
Is it open-air or indoors?	**Ist es ein Freibad oder ein Hallenbad?**	ist ehss ighn frighbart oaderr ighn hahlernbart
Is it heated?	**Ist es geheizt?**	ist ehss gerhightst
Can one swim in the lake/river?	**Kann man im See/Fluß baden?**	kahn mahn im zay/ fluss bardern
I'd like to see a boxing match.	**Ich möchte gern einen Boxkampf sehen.**	ikh murkhter gehrn ighnern bokskahmpf zayern
Can you get me a couple of tickets?	**Können Sie mir zwei Karten besorgen?**	kurnern zee meer tsvigh kahrtern berzorgern
Is there a football (soccer) game anywhere this Saturday?	**Findet diesen Samstag irgendwo ein Fußballspiel statt?**	findert deezern zahmstarg irgerntvoa ighn foosbahlshpeel shtaht
Who's playing?	**Wer spielt?**	vayr shpeelt

Is there any good fishing around here?	**Kann man hier in der Nähe angeln?**	kahn mahn heer in derr naier ahngerln
Do I need a permit?	**Brauche ich einen Angelschein?**	browkher ikh ighnern angerlshighn
Where can I get one?	**Wo bekomme ich einen?**	voa berkommer ikh ighnern

On the beach

Is it safe for swimming?	**Kann man hier ohne Gefahr schwimmen?**	kahn mahn heer oaner gerfarr shvimmern
Is there a lifeguard?	**Gibt es einen Rettungsdienst?**	gipt ehss ighnern rehtungsdeenst
The sea is very calm.	**Die See ist sehr ruhig.**	dee zay ist zayr rooikh
There are some big waves.	**Die See geht recht hoch.**	dee zay gayt rehkht hoakh
Are there any dangerous currents?	**Gibt es gefährliche Strömungen?**	gipt ehss gerfairlikher shtrurmungern
What time is high tide / low tide?	**Wann ist Flut/Ebbe?**	vahn ist floot / ehber
What's the temperature of the water?	**Welche Temperatur hat das Wasser?**	vehlkher tehmperrahtoor haht dahss vahsser
I want to hire a/an...	**Ich möchte... mieten.**	ikh murkhter...meetern
air mattress	**eine Luftmatratze**	ighner luftmahtrahtser
bathing hut	**eine Badekabine**	ighner barderkarbeener
deck-chair	**einen Liegestuhl**	ighnern leegershtool
skin-diving equipment	**eine Tauchausrüstung**	ighner towkhowsrewstung
sunshade	**einen Sonnenschirm**	jghnern zonnernsheerm
surfboard	**ein Brett zum Wellenreiten**	ighn breht tsum vehlernrightern
tent	**ein Zelt**	ighn tsehlt
some water-skis	**Wasserschi**	vahsserrshee

PRIVATSTRAND
PRIVATE BEACH

BADEN VERBOTEN
NO BATHING

RELAXING

Where can I rent a...?	**Wo kann ich... mieten?**	voa kahn ikh...meetern
canoe	**ein Paddelboot**	ighn pahderlboat
motor-boat	**ein Motorboot**	ighn moatorboat
rowing-boat	**ein Ruderboot**	ighn rooderrboat
sailing-boat	**ein Segelboot**	ighn zaygerlboat
What's the charge per hour?	**Was kostet es pro Stunde?**	vahss kostert ehss proa shtunder

Winter sports

Austria and Switzerland are particularly well-known for their ski resorts (some of them operate year round), and both countries contend for the merit of having originated modern skiing. Germany, too, has many well-equipped resorts. For the beginner there are excellent ski schools. Skiing equipment can be hired everywhere, not only in the resorts but also in most sporting goods shops in the cities. Curling, ice-hockey and skating are also widely practiced.

Is there a skating-rink near here?	**Gibt es hier in der Nähe eine Eisbahn?**	gipt ehss heer in derr naier ighner ighsbarn
What are the skiing conditions like at...?	**Wie sind die Schneeverhältnisse in...?**	vee zint dee shnayfehr-hehltnisser in
Can I take skiing lessons there?	**Kann ich dort Schiunterricht nehmen?**	kahn ikh dort sheeunterrikht naymern
Are there ski lifts?	**Gibt es dort Schilifts?**	gipt ehss dort sheelifts
I want to hire a/some...	**Ich möchte... mieten.**	ikh murkhter... meetern
ice skates	**Schlittschuhe**	shlitshooer
skiing equipment	**eine Schiausrüstung**	ighner sheeowssrewstung
toboggan	**einen Rodelschlitten**	ighnern roaderlshlittern
sled	**einen Schlitten**	ighnern shlittern
boots	**Stiefel**	shteeferl
poles	**Schistöcke**	sheesturker
skis	**Schier**	sheeerr

Camping—Countryside

In many parts of Germany, camping isn't allowed without a permit. There are plenty of authorized camping sites, some with excellent facilities.

If you want to be on the safe side, choose a site that is recognized by the ADAC (*Allgemeiner Deutscher Automobil Club*). There are over 700 of them. Switzerland and Austria also have well-equipped camping sites, some of them high up in the mountains. There are numerous youth hostels—for information, apply to the national youth hostels organizations.

If you want to camp on private land, get permission from the owner first.

Can we camp here?	**Können wir hier zelten?**	kurnern veer heer tsehltern
Where can we camp for the night?	**Wo können wir heute nacht zelten?**	voa kurnern veer hoyter nahkht tsehltern
Is there a camping site near here?	**Gibt es hier in der Nähe einen Campingplatz?**	gipt ehss heer in derr nayer ighnern kehmpingplahts
May we camp in your field?	**Dürfen wir auf Ihrer Wiese zelten?**	dewrfern veer owf eererr veezer tsehltern
Can we park our caravan (trailer) here?	**Dürfen wir unseren Wohnwagen hier abstellen?**	dewrfern veer unzerrern voanvargern heer ahpshtehlern
Is this an official camping site?	**Ist dies ein offizieller Campingplatz?**	ist deess ighn ofitsiehlerr kehmpingplahts
May we light a fire?	**Dürfen wir ein Feuer machen?**	dewrfern veer ighn foyerr mahkhern
Is there drinking water?	**Gibt es Trinkwasser?**	gipt ehss trinkvahsserr
Are there shopping facilities on the site?	**Gibt es Einkaufsmöglichkeiten auf dem Platz?**	gipt ehss ighnkowfsmurglikhkightern owf daym plahts

Are there...?	Gibt es...?	gipt ehss
baths	Bäder	baiderr
showers	Duschen	dooshern
toilets	Toiletten	toahlehtern
What's the charge...?	Wie hoch sind die Gebühren...?	vee hoakh zint dee gerbewrern
per day	pro Tag	proa targ
per person	pro Person	proa pehrzoan
for a car	pro Wagen	proa vargern
for a caravan (trailer)	pro Wohnwagen	proa voanvargern
for a tent	pro Zelt	proa tsehlt
Is there a youth hostel near here?	Gibt es hier irgendwo eine Jugendherberge?	gipt ehss heer eergerntvoa ighner yoogernthehrbehrger
Do you know anyone who can put us up for the night?	Kennen Sie jemanden, der uns heute nacht aufnehmen könnte?	kehnern zee yaymahndern derr uns hoyter nahkht owfnaymern kurnter

ZELTEN VERBOTEN	KEINE WOHNWAGEN
NO CAMPING	NO CARAVANS (TRAILERS)

Landmarks

barn	die Scheune	dee shoyner
beach	der Strand	derr shtrahnt
bridge	die Brücke	dee brewker
brook	der Bach	derr bahkh
building	das Gebäude	dahss gerboyder
canal	der Kanal	derr kahnarl
castle	die Burg/das Schloß	dee boorg / dahss shloss
church	die Kirche	dee keerkher
cliff	die Felswand	dee fehlsvahnt
copse	das Gehölz	dahss gerhurlts
cottage	das Häuschen	dahss hoyskhern
crossroads	die Straßenkreuzung	dee shtrarssernkroytsung
farm	der Bauernhof	derr bowerrnhoaf
ferry	die Fähre	dee fairer
field	das Feld	dahss fehlt
footpath	der Fußweg	derr foossvayg
forest	der Wald	derr vahlt
fortress	die Festung	dee fehstung

hamlet	der Weiler	derr **vighlerr**
heath	die Heide	dee **highder**
highway	die Landstraße	dee **lahnts**htrarsser
hill	der Hügel	derr **hewger**l
house	das Haus	dahss howss
hut	die Hütte	dee **hewter**
inn	das Gasthaus	dahss **gahst**howss
lake	der See	derr zay
marsh	das Moor	dahss moar
moorland	das Heidemoor	dahss **high**dermoar
mountain	der Berg	derr behrg
mountain range	die Gebirgskette	dee ger**beergs**kehter
path	der Pfad	derr pfart
peak	die Bergspitze	dee **behrg**shpitser
pond	der Weiher	derr **vigh**err
pool	der Teich	derr tighkh
railway track	das Eisenbahngleis	dahss **igh**zernbarn-glighss
river	der Fluß	derr fluss
road	die Straße	dee **shtrarsser**
ruin	die Ruine	dee **rueener**
sea	die See/das Meer	dee zay/dahss mayr
spring	die Quelle	dee **kvehler**
stream	der Bach	derr bahkh
swamp	der Sumpf	derr zumpf
tower	der Turm	derr toorm
track	der Feldweg	derr **fehlt**vayg
tree	der Baum	derr bowm
valley	das Tal	dahss tarl
village	das Dorf	dahss doarf
vineyard	der Weinberg	derr **vighn**behrg
water	das Gewässer	dahss ger**vehsser**r
waterfall	der Wasserfall	derr **vahsserr**fahl
water tower	der Wasserturm	derr **vahsserr**toorm
well	der Brunnen	derr **brunnern**
wood	der Wald	derr vahlt
What's the name of that river?	Wie heißt dieser Fluß?	vee highst **deezerr** fluss
How high is that mountain?	Wie hoch ist dieser Berg?	vee hoakh ist **deezerr** behrg

...and if you're tired of walking, you can always try hitchhiking—though you may have to wait a long time for a lift.

| Can you give me a lift to...? | Können Sie mich nach ... mitnehmen? | kurnern zee mikh nahkh ...mitnaymern |

FOR ASKING THE WAY, see page 144

Making friends

Introductions

Here are a few phrases to get you started:

How do you do?	**Guten Tag.**	gootern targ
How are you?	**Wie geht es Ihnen?**	vee gayt ehss eenern
Very well, thank you.	**Danke, sehr gut.**	dahngker zayr goot
How's life?	**Wie geht's?**	vee gayts
Fine, thanks. And you?	**Danke gut, und Ihnen?**	dangker goot unt eenern
May I introduce Miss Philips?	**Darf ich Fräulein Philips vorstellen?**	dahrf ikh froylighn Philips foarshtehlern
I'd like you to meet a friend of mine.	**Ich möchte Sie mit einem Freund von mir bekanntmachen.**	ikh murkhter zee mit ighnerm froynt fon meer berkahntmahkhern
John, this is...	**John, das ist...**	John dahss ist
My name's...	**Ich heiße...**	ikh highsser
Glad to know you.	**Sehr erfreut.**	zayr ehrfroyt

Follow-up

How long have you been here?	**Wie lange sind Sie schon hier?**	vee lahnger zint zee shoan heer
We've been here a week.	**Wir sind seit einer Woche hier.**	veer zint zight ighnerr vokher heer
Is this your first visit?	**Ist es Ihr erster Besuch?**	ist ehss eer ehrsterr behzookh
No, we came here last year.	**Nein, wir waren schon letztes Jahr hier.**	nighn veer varrern shoan lehtsterss yarr heer
Are you enjoying your stay?	**Gefällt es Ihnen hier?**	gerfehlt ehss eenern heer

Yes, I like...very much.	**Ja, mir gefällt... sehr gut.**	yar meer ger**fehlt**... zayr goot
Are you on your own?	**Sind Sie allein hier?**	zint zee ah**lighn** heer
I'm with...	**Ich bin mit...**	ikh bin mit
my wife	**meiner Frau**	**migh**nerr frow
my husband	**meinem Mann**	**migh**nerm mahn
my family	**meiner Familie**	**migh**nerr fah**mee**lier
my parents	**meinen Eltern**	**migh**nern **ehl**terrn
some friends	**ein paar Freunden**	ighn parr **froy**ndern
Where do you come from?	**Woher kommen Sie?**	voa**hayr kommern** zee
What part of...do you come from?	**Aus welcher Gegend von... kommen Sie?**	owss **vehl**kherr **gay**gernt fon...**kommern** zee
I'm from...	**Ich bin aus...**	ikh bin owss
Where are you staying?	**Wo wohnen Sie?**	voa **voa**nern zee
I'm a student.	**Ich bin Student.**	ikh bin shtu**ddehnt**
What are you studying?	**Was studieren Sie?**	vahss shtu**ddee**rern zee
We're here on holiday.	**Wir machen Ferien hier.**	veer **mah**khern **fay**riern heer
I'm here on a business trip.	**Ich bin auf einer Geschäftsreise hier.**	ikh bin owf **igh**nerr ger**shehfts**righzer heer
What kind of business are you in?	**In welcher Branche sind Sie?**	in **vehl**kherr **brahngs**her zint zee
What's your occupation?	**Was sind Sie von Beruf?**	vahss zint zee fon berroof
I hope we'll see you again soon.	**Ich hoffe, daß wir Sie bald wiedersehen.**	ikh **hoffer** dahss veer zee bahlt **veederr**zayern
See you later.	**Bis später.**	biss **shpaiterr**
See you tomorrow	**Bis morgen.**	biss **morgern**

The weather

They talk about the weather just as much in Germany as the Americans and British are supposed to do. So…

What a lovely day!	**Was für ein herrlicher Tag!**	vahss fewr ighn hehrlikherr targ
What awful weather.	**Was für ein scheußliches Wetter.**	vahss fewr ighn shoyslikherss vehterr
Isn't it cold today?	**Welche Kälte heute!**	vehlkher kehlter hoyter
Isn't it hot today?	**Welche Hitze heute!**	vehlkher hitser hoyter
Is it usually as warm as this?	**Ist es immer so warm?**	ist ehss immerr zoa vahrm
It's very foggy, isn't it?	**Es ist recht neblig, nicht wahr?**	ehss ist rehkht nayblikh nikht varr
Do you think it'll… tomorrow?	**Glauben Sie, es wird morgen…?**	glowbern zee ehss veert morgern
rain	**regnen**	raygnern
be sunny	**sonnig sein**	sonnikh zighn
snow	**schneien**	shnighern
clear up	**aufklaren**	owfklahrern

Invitations

My wife and I would like you to dine with us on…	**Meine Frau und ich würden Sie gern am…zum Abendessen einladen.**	mighner frow unt ikh vewrdern zee gehrn ahm…tsum arberntehssern ighnlardern
Can you come to dinner tomorrow night?	**Können Sie morgen zum Abendessen kommen?**	kurnern zee morgern tsum arberntehssern kommern
We're giving a small party tomorrow night. I do hope you can come.	**Wir geben morgen abend eine kleine Party. Ich hoffe, Sie können kommen.**	veer gaybern morgern arbent ighner klighner parrtee. ikh hoffer zee kurnern kommern
Can you come over for cocktails this evening?	**Können Sie heute abend auf ein Gläschen zu uns kommen?**	kurnern zee hoyter arbent owf ighn glaiskhern tsu uns kommern

There's a party. Are you coming?	**Es findet eine Party statt. Kommen Sie auch?**	ehss findert ighner parrtee shtaht. kommern zee owkh
That's very kind of you.	**Das ist sehr nett von Ihnen.**	dahss ist zayr neht fon eenern
Great. I'd love to come.	**Prima, ich komme sehr gerne.**	preemar ikh kommer zayr gehrner
What time shall we come?	**Wann sollen wir da sein?**	vahn zollern veer dar zighn
May I bring a friend?	**Kann ich einen Freund mitbringen?**	kahn ikh ighnern froynt mitbringern
May I bring a girl friend?	**Kann ich eine Freundin mitbringen?**	kahn ikh ighner froyndin mitbringern
I'm afraid we've got to go now.	**Leider müssen wir jetzt gehen.**	lighderr mewssern veer yehtst gayern
Next time you must come to visit us.	**Nächstes Mal müssen Sie uns besuchen.**	nehkhsterss marl mewssern zee uns berzookhern
Thanks for the evening. It was great.	**Vielen Dank für den Abend, es war herrlich.**	feelern dahngk fewr dayn arbernt ehss varr hehrlikh

Dating

Would you like a cigarette?	**Darf ich Ihnen eine Zigarette anbieten?**	dahrf ikh eenern ighner tsiggahrehter ahnbeetern
Do you have a light, please?	**Können Sie mir bitte Feuer geben?**	kurnern zee meer bitter foyerr gaybern
Can I get you a drink?	**Darf ich Ihnen etwas zu trinken bestellen?**	dahrf ikh eenern ehtvahss tsu tringkern berstehlern
Excuse me, could you please help me?	**Verzeihung, könnten Sie mir bitte helfen?**	fehrtsighung kurntern zee meer bitter hehlfern
I'm lost. Can you show me the way to…?	**Ich habe mich verlaufen. Können Sie mir den Weg zur/zum … zeigen?**	ikh harber mikh fehrlowfern. kurnern zee meer dayn vayg tsoor / tsum…tsighern
Are you waiting for someone?	**Warten Sie auf jemanden?**	vahrtern zee owf yaymahndern

Are you free this evening?	**Sind Sie heute abend frei?**	zint zee **hoy**ter arbernt frigh
Would you like to go out with me tonight?	**Würden Sie heute abend mit mir ausgehen?**	vewrdern zee **hoy**ter arbernt mit meer **ows**gayern
Would you like to go dancing?	**Würden Sie gern tanzen gehen?**	vewrdern zee gehrn **tahnt**sern **gay**ern
I know a good discotheque.	**Ich kenne eine gute Diskothek.**	ikh **keh**ner **igh**ner **goo**ter disko**a**tayk
Shall we go to the cinema (movies)?	**Wollen wir ins Kino gehen?**	**voll**ern veer ins **kee**noa **gay**ern
Would you like to go for a drive?	**Wollen wir ein bißchen durch die Gegend fahren?**	**voll**ern veer ighn **biss**khern doorkh dee **gay**gernt **far**rern
I'd love to, thank you.	**Danke, sehr gern.**	**dahng**ker zayr gehrn
Where shall we meet?	**Wo treffen wir uns?**	voa **tref**fern veer uns
I'll pick you up at your hotel.	**Ich hole Sie in Ihrem Hotel ab.**	ikh **hoa**ler zee in **eer**erm hoa**tehl** ahp
I'll call for you at 8.	**Ich hole Sie um 8 Uhr ab.**	ikh **hoa**ler zee um 8 oor ahp
May I take you home?	**Darf ich Sie nach Hause bringen?**	dahrf ikh zee nahkh **how**zer **bring**ern
Can I see you again tomorrow?	**Darf ich Sie morgen wiedersehen?**	dahrf ikh zee **mor**gern **vee**derr**zay**ern
Thank you, it's been a wonderful evening.	**Danke, es war ein wunderbarer Abend.**	**dahng**ker ehss varr ighn **vund**err**bar**rerr **ar**bernt
I've enjoyed myself tremendously.	**Ich habe mich sehr gut amüsiert.**	ikh **har**ber mikh zayr goot ahme**wzeert**
What's your telephone number?	**Wie ist Ihre Telefonnummer?**	vee ist **eer**er tehlehfoan-**numm**err
Do you live alone?	**Wohnen Sie allein?**	**voa**nern zee ah**lighn**
What time is your last train?	**Wann geht Ihr letzter Zug?**	vahn gayt eer **lehtst**err tsoog

Shopping guide

This shopping guide is designed to help you find what you
want with ease, accuracy and speed. It features:

1. a list of all major shops, stores and services (p. 98)
2. some general expressions required when shopping to allow
   you to be specific and selective (p. 100)
3. full details of the shops and services most likely to concern
   you. Here you'll find advice, alphabetical lists of items and
   conversion charts listed under the headings below.

SHOPPING GUIDE

Shops, stores and services

If you've a clear idea of what you want before you set out, then look under the appropriate heading, pick out the article and find a suitable description for it (colour, material, etc.).

German shops usually open at around 8 a.m. and close at 6.30 p.m.; some close for lunch. On Saturdays shops close at 1 p.m., except on the first Saturday of the month when they're open until 4 p.m.

In Vienna, shops are open weekdays from 8 or 9 a.m. to 6 p.m., sometimes closing at noon for two or three hours. Stores close at 12.30 p.m. on Saturday. In other Austrian cities, shops often take a lunch break while evening closing hours vary.

Swiss shop hours are usually 8 a.m. to 6.30 p.m. with a two-hour lunch break. In some regions, shops close at 1 p.m. on Saturdays while in other localities shops remain open until 5 p.m.

Where's the nearest...?	Wo ist der/die/das nächste...?	voa ist derr/dee/dahss nehkhster
antique shop	das Antiquitäten-geschäft	dahss ahntikvittaytern-gershehft
art gallery	die Kunstgalerie	dee kunstgahlehree
baker's	die Bäckerei	dee behkerrigh
bank	die Bank	dee bahngk
barber's	der Friseur	derr frizurr
beauty salon	der Kosmetiksalon	derr kosmaytikzahlong
bookshop	die Buchhandlung	dee bukhhahntlung
butcher's	die Fleischerei/ Metzgerei	dee flighsherrigh/ mehtsgerrigh
candy store	der Süßwarenladen	derr sewsvarrernlardern
chemist's	die Apotheke	dee ahpoatayker
confectioner's	die Konditorei	dee konditoarigh
dairy shop	die Milchhandlung	dee milkhhahntlung
delicatessen	das Delikatessen-geschäft	dahss dehlikkahtehssern-gershehft
dentist	der Zahnarzt	derr tsarnahrtst
department store	das Warenhaus	dahss varrernhowss
doctor	der Arzt	derr ahrtst

drugstore	die Apotheke	dee ahpoatayker
dry cleaner's	die chemische Reinigung	dee khaymisher righni-gung
fishmonger's	die Fischhandlung	dee fishhahntlung
furrier's	das Pelzgeschäft	dahss pehltsgershehft
florist's	das Blumengeschäft	dahss bloomerngershehft
greengrocer's	die Gemüsehandlung	dee germewzerhahntlung
grocery	das Lebensmittelgeschäft	dahss laybernsmitterlgershehft
hairdresser's (ladies)	der Damenfriseur	derr darmernfrizurr
hardware store	die Eisenwarenhandlung	dee ighzernvarrernhahntlung
health food shop	das Reformhaus	dahss rehformhowss
hospital	das Krankenhaus	dahss krahngkernhowss
jeweller's	der Juwelier	derr yuvehleer
launderette	der Waschsalon	derr vahshzahlong
laundry	die Wäscherei	dee vehsherrigh
liquor store	die Spirituosenhandlung	dee shpirrituoazernhahntlung
market	der Markt	derr mahrkt
news-stand	der Zeitungsstand	derr tsightungsshtahnt
off-licence	die Spirituosenhandlung	dee shpirrituoazernhahntlung
optician	der Optiker	derr optikkerr
pastry shop	die Konditorei	dee kondittoarigh
photo shop	das Photogeschäft	dahss foatoagershehft
police station	die Polizeiwache	dee politsighvahkher
post office	das Postamt	dahss postahmt
shoe shop	das Schuhgeschäft	dahss shoogershehft
shoemaker's (repairs)	der Schuhmacher	derr shoomahkherr
souvenir shop	der Andenkenladen	derr ahndehngkernlardern
sporting goods shop	das Sportgeschäft	dahss shportgershehft
stationer's	das Schreibwarengeschäft	dahss shrighpvarrerngershehft
supermarket	der Supermarkt	derr zooperrmahrkt
sweet shop	der Süßwarenladen	derr zewsvarrernlardern
tailor's	der Herrenschneider	derr hehrernshnighderr
telegraph office	das Telegraphenamt	dahss tehlehgrarfernahmt
tobacconist's	der Tabakladen	derr tahbahklardern
toy shop	das Spielwarengeschäft	dahss shpeelvarrerngershehft
travel agent	das Reisebüro	dahss righzerbewroa
vegetable store	die Gemüsehandlung	dee germewzerhahntlung
veterinarian	der Tierarzt	derr teerahrtst
watchmaker's	der Uhrmacher	derr oormahkherr
wine merchant's	die Weinhandlung	dee vighnhahntlung

General expressions

Here are some expressions which will be useful to you when you're out shopping:

Where?

Where's a good...?	**Wo ist ein guter...?**	voa ist ighn **goo**terr
Where can I find...?	**Wo finde ich...?**	voa **fin**derr ikh
Where do they sell...?	**Wo bekomme ich...?**	voa ber**kom**merr ikh
Can you recommend an inexpensive...?	**Können Sie einen preiswerten... empfehlen?**	**kur**nern zee **igh**nern **prighs**vayrtern... ehm**fay**lern
Where's the main shopping area?	**Wo ist das Geschäftsviertel?**	voa ist dahss ger**shehfts**feerterl
How far is it from here?	**Wie weit ist es von hier?**	vee vight ist ehss fon heer
How do I get there?	**Wie komme ich dorthin?**	vee **kom**merr ikh **dort**hin

Service

Can you help me?	**Können Sie mir helfen?**	**kur**nern zee meer **hehl**fern
I'm just looking around.	**Ich sehe mich nur um.**	ikh **zay**er mikh noor um
I want...	**Ich hätte gern...**	ikh **heh**ter gehrn
Can you show me some...?	**Können Sie mir einige... zeigen?**	**kur**nern zee meer **igh**nigger...**tsigh**gern
Do you have any...?	**Haben Sie...?**	**har**bern zee

That one

Can you show me...?	**Können Sie mir ... zeigen?**	**kur**nern zee meer ... **tsigh**gern
that/those	**das/diese**	dahss/**dee**zer
the one in the window	**das im Schaufenster**	dahss im **show**fehnsterr
the one in the display case	**das in der Vitrine**	dahss in derr vi**tree**nerr
It's over there.	**Es ist dort drüben.**	ehss ist dort **drew**bern

Defining the article

I'd like a...	**Ich hätte gern...**	ikh **hehter** gehrn
It must be...	**Es muß...sein.**	ehss muss...zighn
big	**groß**	groass
cheap	**billig**	billikh
dark	**dunkel**	dunkerl
good	**gut**	goot
heavy	**schwer**	shvayr
large	**groß**	groass
light (weight)	**leicht**	lighkht
light (colour)	**hell**	hehl
oval	**oval**	oavarl
rectangular	**rechteckig**	rehkhtehkikh
round	**rund**	runt
small	**klein**	klighn
square	**quadratisch**	kvahlittait
I don't want anything too expensive.	**Ich möchte nichts all zu Teures.**	ikh **murkhter** nikhts ahll tsu **toyrerss**

Preference

I prefer something of better quality.	**Ich hätte lieber eine bessere Qualität.**	ikh **hehter leeberr ighner behsserer** kvahlit**tait**
Can you show me some more?	**Können Sie mir bitte mehr zeigen?**	kurnern zee meer **bitter** mayr tsighgern
Haven't you anything...?	**Haben Sie nicht etwas...?**	harbern zee nikht ehtvahss
cheaper/better	**Billigeres/Besseres**	billigerrerss / behsserrerss
larger/smaller	**Größeres/Kleineres**	grursserrerss / klighnerrerss

How much?

How much is this?	**Wieviel kostet das?**	veefeel kostert dahss
How much are they?	**Wieviel kosten sie?**	veefeel kostern zee
I don't understand.	**Ich verstehe nicht.**	ikh fehrshtayer nikht
Please write it down.	**Schreiben Sie es bitte auf.**	shrighbern zee ehss bitter owf
I don't want to spend more than 20 marks.	**Ich möchte nicht mehr als 20 Mark ausgeben.**	ikh **murkhter** nikht mayr ahls 20 mahrk **ows**gaybern

FOR COLOURS, see page 113

SHOPPING GUIDE

Decision

That's just what I want.	**Das ist genau das, was ich möchte.**	dahss ist gernow dahss vahss ikh murkhter
It's not quite what I want.	**Es ist nicht ganz das, was ich möchte.**	ehss ist nikht gahnts dahss vahss ikh murkhter
No, I don't like it.	**Nein, das gefällt mir nicht.**	nighn dahss gerfehlt meer nikht
I'll take it.	**Ich nehme es.**	ikh naymer ehss

Ordering

Can you order it for me?	**Können Sie es mir bestellen?**	kurnern zee ehss meer bershtehlern
How long will it take?	**Wie lange dauert es?**	vee lahnger dowerrt ehss
I'd like it as soon as possible.	**Ich hätte es gern so schnell wie möglich.**	ikh hehter ehss gehrn zoa shnehl vee murglikh

Delivery

I'll take it with me.	**Ich nehme es mit.**	ikh naymer ehss mit
Deliver it to the... Hotel.	**Liefern Sie es bitte ins Hotel...**	leeferrn zee ehss bitter ins hoatehl
Please send it to this address.	**Senden Sie es bitte an diese Adresse.**	zehndern zee ehss bitter ahn deezer ahdrehsser
Will I have any difficulty with customs?	**Werde ich Schwierigkeiten mit dem Zoll haben?**	vayrder ikh shveerikhkightern mit daym tsol harbern

Paying

How much is it?	**Wieviel kostet es?**	veefeel kostert ehss
Can I pay by traveller's cheque?	**Kann ich mit einem Reisescheck bezahlen?**	kahn ikh mit ighnerm righzershehk bertsarlern
Do you accept dollars / pounds?	**Nehmen Sie Dollar/ Pfund an?**	naymern zee dollahr/ pfunt ahn
Do you accept credit cards?	**Nehmen Sie Kreditkarten an?**	naymern zee krayditkahrtern ahn

Haven't you made a mistake in the bill?	Haben Sie sich nicht verrechnet?	harbern zee zikh nikht fehrrehkhnert
Do you have a carrier (shopping) bag?	Haben Sie eine Tragetasche?	harbern zee ighner trargertahsher
Would you please gift wrap it?	Würden Sie es bitte als Geschenk einpacken?	vewrdern zee ehss bitter ahlss gershehngk ighnpahkern

Dissatisfied

Can you please exchange this?	Können Sie das bitte umtauschen?	kurnern zee dahss bitter umtowshern
I want to return this.	Ich möchte das zurückgeben.	ikh murkhter dahss tsoorewkgaybern
I'd like a refund. Here's the receipt.	Ich möchte das Geld zurückerstattet haben. Hier ist die Quittung.	ikh murkhter dahss gehlt tsoorewkehrshtahtert harbern. heer ist dee kvittung

Kann ich Ihnen helfen?	Can I help you?
Was hätten Sie gerne?	What would you like?
Welche...möchten Sie?	What...would you like?
Farbe/Form Qualität/Menge	colour/shape quality/quantity
Es tut mir leid, das haben wir nicht.	I'm sorry, we haven't any.
Das haben wir nicht vorrätig.	We're out of stock.
Sollen wir es für Sie bestellen?	Shall we order it for you?
Nehmen Sie es mit oder sollen wir es Ihnen senden?	Will you take it with you or shall we send it?
Sonst noch etwas?	Anything else?
Das macht...Mark, bitte.	That's...marks, please.
Die Kasse ist dort drüben.	The cashier's over there.

Bookshop—Stationer's—News-stand

In Germany, bookshops and stationers' are usually separate shops, though the latter will often sell paperbacks. Newspapers and magazines are sold at news-stands.

Where's the nearest...?	**Wo ist der/die/ das nächste...?**	voa ist derr/dee/dahss **neh**khster
bookshop	**die Buchhandlung**	dee bukh**hahn**tlung
stationer's	**das Schreibwaren- geschäft**	dahss **shrighp**varrern- gershehft
news-stand	**der Zeitungsstand**	derr **tsigh**tungsshtahnt
Where can I buy an English-language newspaper?	**Wo kann ich eine englische Zeitung bekommen?**	voa kahn ikh **igh**ner **ehng**lisher **tsigh**tung ber**kom**mern
I want to buy a/an/some...	**Ich möchte...**	ikh **murkh**ter
address book	**ein Adressen- büchlein**	ighn ah**dreh**ssern- bewkhlighn
ball-point pen	**einen Kugel- schreiber**	**igh**nern **koo**gerlshrighberr
book	**ein Buch**	ighn bukh
box of paints	**einen Farbkasten**	**igh**nern **fahrp**kahstern
carbon paper	**Durchschlagpapier**	**doorkh**shlargpahpeer
cellophane tape	**durchsichtigen Klebestreifen**	**doorkh**sikhtiggern **klay**bershtrighfern
crayons	**Farbstifte**	**fahrp**shtifter
dictionary	**ein Wörterbuch**	ighn **vurr**terrbookh
German-English	**deutsch-englisch**	doych-**ehng**lish
pocket dictionary	**ein Taschen- wörterbuch**	ighn **tah**shernvurrterr- bookh
drawing paper	**Zeichenpapier**	**tsigh**khernpahpeer
drawing pins	**Reißwecken**	**righst**svehkern
envelopes	**Briefumschläge**	**breef**umshlaiger
eraser	**einen Radiergummi**	**igh**nern rah**deer**gummi
exercise book	**ein Schreibheft**	ighn **shrighp**heft
fountain pen	**einen Füllfederhalter**	**igh**nern fewl**fay**derrhahlterr
glue	**Leim**	lighm
grammar book	**eine Grammatik**	**igh**ner grah**mah**tik
guide-book	**einen Reiseführer**	**igh**nern **righ**zerfewrerr
ink	**Tinte**	**tin**ter
black/red/blue	**schwarz/rot/blau**	shvahrts/roat/blow
labels	**Etikette**	**eh**tikehter
magazine	**eine Illustrierte**	**igh**ner illu**streer**ter

map	eine Landkarte	ighner lahntkahrter
map of the town	einen Stadtplan	ighnern shtahtplarn
road map of...	eine Straßenkarte von...	ighner shtrarssernkahrter fon
newspaper	eine Zeitung	ighner tsightung
American	amerikanische	ahmehrikarnisher
English	englische	ehnglisher
notebook	ein Notizheft	ighn nottitshehft
note paper	Briefpapier	breefpahpeer
paperback	ein Taschenbuch	ighn tahshernbookh
paper napkins	Papierservietten	pahpeerzehrviehtern
paste	Klebstoff	klaybshtof
pen	eine Feder	ighner fayderr
pencil	einen Bleistift	ighnern blighshtift
pencil sharpener	einen Bleistift- spitzer	ighnern blighshtiftshpitserr
playing cards	Spielkarten	shpeelkahrtern
postcards	Postkarten	postkahrtern
rubber	einen Radiergummi	ighnern rahdeergummi
ruler	ein Lineal	ighn linneharl
sketching pad	einen Zeichenblock	ighnern tsighkhernblok
string	Bindfaden/Schnur	bintfardern/shnoor
thumbtacks	Reißzwecken	righstsvehkern
tissue paper	Seidenpapier	zighdernpahpeer
tracing paper	Pauspapier	powspahpeer
typewriter ribbon	ein Farbband	ighn fahrpbahnt
typing paper	Schreibmaschinen- papier	shrighpmahsheenern- pahpeer
writing pad	einen Schreibblock	ighnern shrighpblok
Where's the guide- book section?	Wo stehen die Reiseführer?	voa shtayern dee righzerfewrerr
Where do you keep the English books?	Wo stehen die englischen Bücher?	voa shtayern dee ehnglishern bewkherr
Have you any of...'s books in English?	Haben Sie ein Buch von...in Englisch?	harbern zee ighn bookh fon ... in ehnglish

Here are some contemporary German authors whose books are available in English translation:

Ingeborg Bachmann (Austrian)
Heinrich Böll
Friedrich Dürrenmatt (Swiss)
Max Frisch (Swiss)
Günter Grass

Uwe Johnson
Ernst Jünger
Siegfried Lenz
Martin Walser
Carl Zuckmayer

Camping

Here we're concerned with the equipment you may need.

I'd like a/an/some...	Ich möchte...	ikh murkhter
axe	eine Axt	ighner ahkst
bottle-opener	einen Flaschenöffner	ighnern flahshernurfnerr
bucket	einen Eimer	ighnern ighmerr
butane gas	Butangas	buttarngahss
camp bed	ein Feldbett	ighn fehltbeht
camping equipment	eine Campingaus-rüstung	ighner kehmpingows-rewstung
can opener	einen Büchsenöffner	ighnern bewksernurfnerr
candles	Kerzen	kehrtsern
chair	einen Stuhl	ighnern shtool
folding chair	Klappstuhl	klahpshtool
compass	einen Kompaß	ighnern kompahss
corkscrew	einen Korkenzieher	ighnern korkerntseeherr
crockery	Geschirr	gersheer
cutlery	Besteck	bershtehk
deck-chair	einen Liegestuhl	ighnern leegershtool
first-aid kit	einen Verbandkasten	ighnern fehrbahntkahstern
fishing tackle	Angelzeug	ahngerltsoyg
flashlight	eine Taschenlampe	ighner tahshernlahmper
frying-pan	eine Bratpfanne	ighner brartpfaner
groundsheet	einen Zeltboden	ighnern tsehltboadern
hammer	einen Hammer	ighnern hahmerr
hammock	eine Hängematte	ighner hehngermahter
haversack	eine Provianttasche	ighner proaviahnttahsher
ice-bag	einen Eisbehälter	ighnern ighsberhehlterr
kerosene	Petroleum	paytroalayum
kettle	einen Kessel	ighnern kehsserl
knapsack	einen Tornister	ighnern tornisterr
lamp	eine Lampe	ighner lahmper
lantern	eine Laterne	ighner lahtehrner
matches	Streichhölzer	shtrighkhhurltserr
mattress	eine Matratze	ighner mahtrahtser
methylated spirits	Brennspiritus	brehnshpeerittuss
pail	einen Eimer	ighnern ighmerr
paraffin	Petroleum	paytroalayum
penknife	ein Taschenmesser	ighn tahshernmehsserr
picnic case	einen Picknickkoffer	ighnern piknik-kofferr
pressure cooker	einen Dampf-kochtopf	ighnern dahmpfkokhtopf
primus stove	einen Primuskocher	ighnern preemuskokherr
rope	ein Seil	ighn zighl

rucksack	einen Rucksack	ighnern rukzahk
saucepan	einen Kochtopf	ighnern kokhtopf
scissors	eine Schere	ighner shayrer
screwdriver	einen Schrauben-zieher	ighnern shrowberntseeherr
sheathknife	ein Fahrtenmesser	ighn farrternmehsserr
sleeping bag	einen Schlafsack	ighnern shlarfzahk
stewpan	einen Schmortopf	ighnern shmoartopf
stove	einen Kocher	ighnern kokherr
table	einen Tisch	ighnern tish
folding table	Klapptisch	klahptish
tent	ein Zelt	ighn tsehlt
tent-pegs	Heringe	hayringer
tent-pole	eine Zeltstange	ighner tsehltshtahnger
thermos flask (bottle)	eine Thermosflasche	ighner tehrmosflahsher
tin-opener	einen Büchsenöffner	ighnern bewksernurfnerr
tongs	eine Zange	ighner tsahnger
tool kit	einen Werkzeug-kasten	ighnern vehrktsoygkahstern
torch	eine Taschenlampe	ighner tahshernlahmper
water carrier	einen Wasser-kanister	ighnern vahsserrkahnisterr
wood alcohol	Brennspiritus	brehnshpeerittuss

Crockery

cups	die Tassen	dee tahssern
food box	die Proviantkiste	dee proaviahntkister
mugs	die Becher	dee behkherr
plates	die Teller	dee tehlerr
saucers	die Untertassen	dee unterrtahssern

Cutlery

forks	die Gabeln	dee garberln
knives	die Messer	dee mehsserr
dessert knives	die Dessertmesser	dee dehssayrmehsserr
spoons	die Löffel	dee lurferl
teaspoons	die Teelöffel	dee taylurferl
(made of) plastic	(aus) Plastik	(owss) plahstik
(made of) stainless steel	(aus) rostfreiem Stahl	(owss) rostfrigherm shtarl

Chemist's—Drugstore

In German, a chemist's (drugstore) is called *Apotheke* (ahpo-**tay**ker). These don't sell cameras, books and the like. If you're looking for toiletries, household articles or film, try a *Drogerie* (droge**hree**). You'll also find non-prescription medicine available in a *Drogerie*.

This section has been divided into two parts:

1. Pharmaceutical—medicine, first-aid, etc.
2. Toiletry—toilet articles, cosmetics

General

Where's the nearest (all-night) chemist's?	**Wo ist die nächste Apotheke (mit Nachtdienst)?**	voa ist dee **nehkh**ster ahpoa**tay**ker (mit **nahkht**deenst)
What time does the chemist's open / close?	**Um wieviel Uhr öffnet/schließt die Apotheke?**	um **vee**feel oor **urf**nert/**shleest** dee ahpoa**tay**ker

Part 1—Pharmaceutical

I want something for...	**Ich möchte etwas gegen...**	ikh **murkh**ter **eht**vahss **gay**gern
a cold	**eine Erkältung**	**igh**ner ehr**kehl**tung
a cough	**Husten**	**hoos**tern
a hangover	**Kater**	**kar**terr
hay fever	**Heuschnupfen**	**hoy**shnupfern
sunburn	**Sonnenbrand**	**sonnen**brahnt
travel sickness	**Reisekrankheit**	**righ**zerkrahnk-hight
an upset stomach	**Magenverstimmung**	**mar**gernfehrshtimmung
Can you make up this prescription for me?	**Können Sie mir dieses Rezept machen?**	**kur**nern zee meer **dee**zerss reh**tsehpt** **mahkh**ern
Shall I wait?	**Soll ich warten?**	zol ikh **vahr**tern
When shall I come back?	**Wann kann ich zurückkommen?**	vahn kahn ikh tsoo**rewk**kommern
Can I get it without a prescription?	**Kann ich das ohne Rezept bekommen?**	kahn ikh dahss **oa**ner reh**tsehpt** ber**kommern**

FOR DOCTOR, see page 162

Can I have a/an/ some...?	Kann ich...haben?	kahn ikh...harbern
ammonia	**Ammoniak**	ahmonniahk
antiseptic cream	**eine Wundsalbe**	ighner vuntzahlber
aspirin	**Aspirin**	ahspeereen
bandage	**einen Verband**	ighnern fehrbahnt
crepe bandage	**eine elastische Binde**	ighner ehlahstisher binder
gauze bandage	**eine Mullbinde**	ighner mulbinder
Band-Aids	**Heftpflaster**	hehftpflahsterr
calcium tablets	**Kalktabletten**	kahlktahblehtern
castor oil	**Rizinusöl**	ritsinnussurl
chlorine tablets	**Chlortabletten**	kloartahblehtern
contraceptive	**ein Verhütungsmittel**	ighn fehrhewtungsmitterl
corn plasters	**Hühneraugenpflaster**	hewnerrowgernpflahsterr
cotton wool	**Watte**	vahter
cough drops	**Hustenbonbons**	hoosternbongbong
diabetic lozenges	**Diabetikerpastillen**	diahbaytikkerrpahstillern
disinfectant	**ein Desinfektionsmittel**	ighn dehsinfehktsioansmitterl
ear drops	**Ohrentropfen**	oarerntropfern
Elastoplast	**Heftpflaster**	hehftpflahsterr
eye drops	**Augentropfen**	owgerntropfern
first-aid kit	**einen Verbandkasten**	ighnern fehrbahntkahstern
gargle	**Gurgelwasser**	goorgerlvahsserr
gauze	**Verbandmull**	fehrbahntmul
insect lotion	**ein Insektenmittel**	ighn inzehkternmitterl
iodine	**Jod**	yoat
iron pills	**Eisentabletten**	ighzerntahblehtern
laxative	**ein Abführmittel**	ighn ahpfewrmitterl
lint	**Verbandmull**	fehrbahntmul
mouthwash	**Mundwasser**	muntvahsserr
sanitary napkins	**Damenbinden**	darmernbindern
sedative	**ein Beruhigungsmittel**	ighn berrooigungsmitterl
sleeping pills	**Schlaftabletten**	shlarftahblehtern
stomach pills	**Magentabletten**	margerntahblehtern
thermometer	**ein Thermometer**	ighn thermommayterr
throat lozenges	**Halspastillen**	hahlspahstillern
tonic	**ein Stärkungsmittel**	ighn shtehrkungsmitterl
vitamin pills	**Vitamintabletten**	vittahmeentahblehtern
weight-reducing tablets	**Schlankheitspillen**	shlahngkhightspillern

SHOPPING GUIDE

Part 2—Toiletry

I'd like a/an some...	Ich hätte gerne...	ikh hehter gehrner
acne cream	eine Aknesalbe	ighner ahknerzahlber
after-shave lotion	ein Rasierwasser	ighn rahzeervahsserr
astringent	ein Adstringens	ighn ahdstringehns
bath essence	Badeessenz	barderehssehnts
bath salts	Badesalz	barderzahlts
cologne	ein Kölnischwasser	ighn kurlnishvahsserr
cream	eine Creme	ighner kraym
cleansing cream	Reinigungscreme	righniggungskraym
cuticle cream	Nagelhautcreme	nargerlhowtkraym
enzyme cream	Enzymcreme	ehntsewmkraym
hormone cream	Hormoncreme	hormoankraym
moisturizing cream	Feuchtigkeitscreme	foykhtikhkightskraym
night cream	Nachtcreme	nahkhtkraym
cuticle remover	Nagelhautentferner	nargerlhowtehntfehrnerr
deodorant	ein Desodorans	ighn dehzoadoarahns
emery board	eine Sandpapierfeile	ighner zahntpahpeerfighler
eye liner	einen Lidstift	ighnern leedshtift
eye pencil	einen Augenbrauen-stift	ighnern owgernbrowern-shtift
eye shadow	einen Lidschatten	ighnern leedshahtern
face pack	eine Gesichtsmaske	ighner gerzikhtsmahsker
face powder	Gesichtspuder	gerzikhtspooderr
foot cream	Fußcreme	fooskraym
foot powder	Fußpuder	foospooderr
hand cream	Handcreme	hahntkraym
hand lotion	Handlotion	hahntlotsioan
lipsalve	eine Lippenpomade	ighner lippernpommarder
lipstick	einen Lippenstift	ighnern lippernshtift
lipstick brush	einen Lippenpinsel	ighnern lippernpinzerl
make-up bag	einen Kosmetik-beutel	ighnern kosmaytikboyterl
make-up remover pads	Abschminkwatte	ahpshmingkvahter
mascara	Wimperntusche	vimperrntusher
nail brush	eine Nagelbürste	ighner nargerlbewrster
nail clippers	eine Nagelzange	ighner nargerltsahnger
nail file	eine Nagelfeile	ighner nargerlfighler
nail polish	Nagellack	nargerllahk
nail polish remover	Nagellackentferner	nargerllahkehntfehrnerr
nail scissors	eine Nagelschere	ighner nargerlshayrer
perfume	ein Parfüm	ighn pahrfewm
powder	Puder	pooderr
pumice stone	einen Bimsstein	ighnern bimsshtighn
razor	einen Rasierapparat	ighnern rahzeerahpahrart

razor blades	**Rasierklingen**	rahzeerklingern
rouge	**Rouge**	roozh
safety pins	**Sicherheitsnadeln**	zikherrhightsnarderln
shampoo	**ein Haarwaschmittel**	ighn harrvahshmitterl
shaving brush	**einen Rasierpinsel**	ighnern rahzeerpinzerl
shaving cream	**Rasiercreme**	rahzeerkraym
shaving soap	**Rasierseife**	rahzeerzighfer
soap	**eine Seife**	ighner zighfer
sponge	**einen Schwamm**	ighnern shvahm
sun-tan cream	**Sonnencreme**	sonnernkraym
sun-tan oil	**Sonnenöl**	sonnernurl
talcum powder	**Talkumpuder**	tahlkumpooderr
tissues	**Papiertücher**	pahpeertewkherr
toilet paper	**Toilettenpapier**	toaahlehternpahpeer
toilet water	**ein Toilettenwasser**	ighn toaahlehternvahsserr
toothbrush	**eine Zahnbürste**	ighner tsarnbewrster
toothpaste	**Zahnpasta**	tsarnpahstar
toothpowder	**Zahnpuder**	tsarnpooderr
tweezers	**eine Pinzette**	ighner pintsehter

For your hair

bobby pins	**Haarklemmen**	harrklehmern
brush	**eine Haarbürste**	ighner harrbewrster
comb	**einen Kamm**	ighnern kahm
dye	**ein Färbemittel**	ighn fehrbermitterl
grips	**Haarklips**	harrklips
lacquer	**einen Haarlack**	ighnern harrlahk
oil	**ein Haaröl**	ighn harrurl
pins	**Haarnadeln**	harrnarderln
rollers	**Lockenwickler**	lokkernviklerr
setting lotion	**einen Haarfestiger**	ighnern harrfehstigerr
tint	**ein Tönungsmittel**	ighn turnungsmitterl

For the baby

bib	**ein Lätzchen**	ighn lehtskhern
diapers (nappies)	**Windeln**	vinderln
diaper pins	**Windelklammern**	vinderlklahmerrn
dummy (pacifier)	**einen Schnuller**	ighnern shnullerr
plastic pants	**ein Plastikhöschen**	ighn plahstikhurskhern

Clothing

If you want to buy something specific, prepare yourself in advance. Look at the list of clothing on page 117. Get some idea of the colour, material and size you want. They're all listed on the next few pages.

General

I'd like...	**Ich möchte...**	ikh murkhter
I want...for a 10-year-old boy.	**Ich möchte...für einen 10-jährigen Jungen.**	ikh murkhter ... fewr ighnern 10-yairiggern yungern
I want something like this.	**Ich möchte etwas in dieser Art.**	ikh murkhter ehtvahss in deezerr arrt
I like the one in the window.	**Das im Schaufenster gefällt mir.**	dahss im showfehnsterr gerfehlt meer
How much is that per metre?	**Wieviel kostet der Meter?**	veefeel kostert derr mayterr

1 centimetre = 0.39 in.	1 inch = 2.54 cm.
1 metre = 39.37 in.	1 foot = 30.5 cm.
10 metres = 32.81 ft.	1 yard = 0.91 m.

Colour

I want something in...	**Ich möchte etwas in...**	ikh murkhter ehtvahss in
I want a darker shade.	**Ich möchte es etwas dunkler.**	ikh murkhter ehss ehtvahss dungklerr
I want something to match this.	**Ich möchte etwas hierzu Passendes.**	ikh murkhter ehtvahss heertsoo pahssernderss
I don't like the colour.	**Die Farbe gefällt mir nicht.**	dee fahrber gerfehlt meer nikht

uni	gestreift	gepunktet	kariert	gemustert
(unni)	(gershtrighft)	(gerpungktert)	(kahreert)	(germusterrt)

beige	**beige**	bayzh
black	**schwarz**	shvahrts
blue	**blau**	blow
brown	**braun**	brown
cream	**creme**	kraym
crimson	**karmin-rot**	kahrmeen-roat
emerald	**smaragdgrün**	smahrahgtgrewn
fawn	**hellbraun**	hehlbrown
gold	**golden**	goldern
green	**grün**	grewn
grey	**grau**	grow
mauve	**lila**	leelah
orange	**orangenfarben**	oarahngzhernfahrbern
pink	**rosa**	roazah
purple	**purpurrot**	poorpoorroat
red	**rot**	roat
scarlet	**scharlachrot**	shahrlahkhroat
silver	**silbern**	zilbern
tan	**bräunlich**	broynlikh
turquoise	**türkisfarben**	tewrkeesfahrbern
white	**weiß**	vighss
yellow	**gelb**	gehlp

Material

Do you have anything in...?	**Haben Sie etwas in...?**	harbern zee ehtvahss in
I want a cotton blouse.	**Ich möchte eine Baumwollbluse.**	ikh murkhter ighner bowmvolbloozer
Is that...?	**Ist das...?**	ist dahss
hand-made	**Handarbeit**	hahntahrbight
imported	**importiert**	importeert
made here	**inländisches Fabrikat**	inlehndisherss fahbrikkart
I want something thinner.	**Ich möchte etwas Dünneres.**	ikh murkhter ehtvahss dewnerrerss
Do you have any better quality?	**Haben Sie eine bessere Qualität?**	harbern zee ighner behsserer kvahlitait
What's it made of?	**Welches Material ist das?**	vehlkherss mahtehriarl ist dahss

It may be made of...

cambric	**Batist**	bahtist
camel-hair	**Kamelhaar**	kahmaylharr
chiffon	**Chiffon**	shiffoan
corduroy	**Kord**	kort
cotton	**Baumwolle**	bowmvoller
crepe	**Krepp**	krehp
denim	**Drillich**	drillikh
felt	**Filz**	filts
flannel	**Flanell**	flahnehl
gabardine	**Gabardine**	gahbahrdin
lace	**Spitze**	shpitser
leather	**Leder**	layderr
linen	**Leinen**	lighnern
needlecord	**Feinkord**	fighnkort
piqué	**Pikee**	pikkay
poplin	**Popeline**	popperleen
rayon	**Kunstseide**	kunstsighder
satin	**Satin**	sahtehng
silk	**Seide**	zighder
suede	**Wildleder**	viltlayderr
taffeta	**Taft**	tahft
terrycloth	**Frottee**	frottay
tulle	**Tüll**	tewl
tweed	**Tweed**	tveet
velvet	**Samt**	zahmt
velveteen	**Manchester**	mahnshehsterr
velour	**Velours**	vehloor
wool	**Wolle**	voller
worsted	**Kammgarn**	kahmgahrn
synthetic	**synthetisch**	zewntaytish
wash and wear	**bügelfrei**	bewgerlfrigh
wrinkle-resistant	**knitterfrei**	knitterrfrigh

Size

My size is 38.	**Ich habe Größe 38.**	ikh harber grursser 38
I don't know your sizes. Could you measure me?	**Ich kenne Ihre Größen nicht. Können Sie mir Maß nehmen?**	ikh kehner eerer grussern nikht. kurnern zee meer mahss naymern

If you don't know continental sizes, consult the charts on the next page.

This is your size

In Europe as in Britain and the U.S., sizes vary somewhat
from country to country. These charts should therefore be
considered as an approximate guide.

Ladies

Dresses/Suits					
American ⎱	10	12	14	16	18	20
British ⎰	32	34	36	38	40	42
Continental	38	40	42	44	46	48

Stockings							Shoes			
American ⎱	8	8½	9	9½	10	10½	6	7	8	9
British ⎰							4½	5½	6½	7½
Continental	0	1	2	3	4	5	37	38	40	41

Gentlemen

Suits/Overcoats							Shirts			
American ⎱	36	38	40	42	44	46	15	16	17	18
British ⎰										
Continental	46	48	50	52	54	56	38	41	43	45

Shoes									
American ⎱	5	6	7	8	8½	9	9½	10	11
British ⎰									
Continental	38	39	41	42	43	43	44	44	45

A good fit?

Can I try it on?	**Kann ich es anprobieren?**	kahn ikh ehss ahnproabeerern
Where's the fitting room?	**Wo ist die Umkleidekabine?**	voa ist dee umklighderkahbeener
Is there a mirror?	**Hat es einen Spiegel?**	haht ehss ighnern shpeegerl
Does it fit?	**Paßt es?**	pahst ehss

FOR NUMBERS, see page 175

It fits very well.	**Es paßt ausgezeichnet.**	ehss pahst **owsger-tsighkhnert**
It doesn't fit.	**Es paßt nicht.**	ehss pahst nikht
It's too...	**Es ist zu...**	ehss ist tsu
short/long	**kurz/lang**	koorts/lahng
tight/loose	**eng/weit**	ehng/vight
How long will it take to alter?	**Wie lange brauchen Sie, um es zu ändern?**	vee **lahnger browkhern** zee um ehss tsu **ehnderrn**

Shoes

I'd like a pair of...	**Ich möchte ein Paar...**	ikh **murkhter** ighn parr
shoes/sandals	**Schuhe/Sandalen**	shooer/zahndarlern
boots/slippers	**Stiefel/Hausschuhe**	shteeferl/howsshooer
These are too...	**Diese sind zu...**	deezer zint tsu
narrow/wide	**eng/weit**	ehng/vight
large/small	**groß/klein**	groass/klighn
They pinch my toes.	**Sie drücken an den Zehen.**	zee drewkern ahn dayn tsayern
Do you have a larger size?	**Haben Sie eine größere Nummer?**	harbern zee ighner grursserrer nummerr
I want a smaller size.	**Ich möchte eine kleinere Nummer.**	ikh murkhter ighner klighnerrer nummerr
Do you have the same in...?	**Haben Sie die gleichen in...?**	harbern zee dee glighkhern in
brown/beige	**braun/beige**	brown/bayzh
black/white	**schwarz/weiß**	shvahrts/vighss

Shoes worn out? Here's the key to getting them fixed again:

Can you repair these shoes?	**Können Sie diese Schuhe reparieren?**	kurnern zee deezer shooer rehpahreerern
Can you stitch this?	**Können Sie das nähen?**	kurnern zee dahss naiern
I want new soles and heels.	**Ich möchte neue Sohlen und Absätze.**	ikh murkhter noyer zoalern unt ahpzehtser
When will they be ready?	**Wann sind sie fertig?**	vahn zint zee fehrtikh

Clothes and accessories

I'd like a/an/some...	Ich hätte gerne...	ikh hehter gehrner
anorak	einen Anorak	ighnern ahnorrahk
bath robe	einen Bademantel	ighnern bardermahnterl
blazer	einen Blazer	ighnern blayzerr
blouse	eine Bluse	ighner bloozer
bow tie	eine Fliege	ighner fleeger
bra	einen Büstenhalter	ighnern bewsternhahlterr
braces	Hosenträger	hoazerntraigerr
briefs	eine kurze Unterhose	ighner koortser unterrhoazer
cap	eine Mütze	ighner mewtser
cardigan	eine Wollweste	ighner volvehster
coat	einen Mantel	ighnern mahnterl
dinner jacket	einen Smoking	ighnern smoaking
dress	ein Kleid	ighn klight
dressing gown	einen Morgenrock	ighnern morgenrrok
evening dress	ein Abendkleid	ighn arberntklight
frock	ein Kleid	ighn klight
fur coat	einen Pelzmantel	ighnern pehltsmahnterl
garter belt	einen Strumpfgürtel	ighnern shtrumpfgewrterl
girdle	einen Hüfthalter	ighnern hewfthahlterr
gloves	Handschuhe	hahntshooer
gym shoes	Turnschuhe	toornshooer
handkerchief	ein Taschentuch	ighn tahsherntookh
hat	einen Hut	ighnern hoot
housecoat	einen Hausmantel	ighnern howsmahnterl
jacket	ein Jackett/eine Jacke	ighn zhahkeht/ighner yahker
jeans	Jeans	"jeans"
jersey	eine Strickjacke	ighner shtrikyahker
jumper (Br.)	einen Pullover	ighnern pulloaverr
jumper (Am.)	einen Trägerrock	ighnern traigerrrok
leather trousers	eine Lederhose	ighner layderrhoazer
lingerie	Unterwäsche	unterrvehsher
mackintosh	einen Regenmantel	ighnern raygernmahnterl
negligé	ein Negligé	ighn nehglizhay
nightdress	ein Nachthemd	ighn nahkhthehmt
overcoat	einen Mantel	ighnern mahnterl
pair of...	ein Paar...	ighn parr
panties	einen Schlüpfer	ighnern shlewpferr
pants	eine Hose	ighner hoazer
pants suit	einen Hosenanzug	ighnern hoazernahntsoog
panty-girdle	ein Strumpf- halterhöschen	ighn shtrumpfhahlterr- hurskhern

panty hose	eine Strumpfhose	ighner shtrumpfhoazer
parka	einen Anorak	ighnern ahnoarahk
pullover	einen Pullover	ighnern pulloaverr
pyjamas	einen Schlafanzug	ighnern shlarfahntsoog
raincoat	einen Regenmantel	ighnern raygernmahnterl
scarf	ein Halstuch	ighn hahlstookh
shirt	ein Hemd	ighn hehmt
shoes	Schuhe	shooer
shorts	Shorts	"shorts"
skirt	einen Rock	ighnern rok
slip	einen Unterrock	ighnern unterrrok
slippers	Hausschuhe	howsshooer
socks	Socken	zokkern
sports jacket	eine Sportjacke	ighner shportyahker
stockings	Strümpfe	shtrewmpfer
suit (man's)	einen Anzug	ighnern ahntsoog
suit (woman's)	ein Kostüm	ighn kostewm
suspender belt	einen Strumpfgürtel	ighnern shtrumpfgewrterl
suspenders (Am.)	Hosenträger	hoazerntraigerr
sweater	einen Pullover	ighnern pulloaverr
swimsuit	einen Badeanzug	ighnern barderahntsoog
T-shirt	ein T-Shirt	ighn "T-shirt"
tennis shoes	Tennisschuhe	tehnisshooer
tie	eine Krawatte	ighner krahvahter
top coat	einen Überzieher	ighnern ewberrtseeherr
track suit	einen Trainings-anzug	ighnern trainingsahntsoog
trousers	eine Hose	ighner hoazer
underpants (men)	eine Unterhose	ighner unterrhoazer
undershirt	ein Unterhemd	ighn unterrhehmt
vest (Am.)	eine Weste	ighner vehster
vest (Br.)	ein Unterhemd	ighn unterrhehmt
waistcoat	eine Weste	ighner vehster

belt	der Gürtel	derr gewrterl
buckle	die Schnalle	dee shnaller
button	der Knopf	derr knopf
collar	der Kragen	derr krargern
cuffs	die Manschetten	dee mahnshehtern
elastic	das Gummiband	dahss gummibahnt
pocket	die Tasche	dee tahsher
shoe laces	die Schnürsenkel	dee shnewrzehnkerl
sleeve	der Ärmel	derr airmerl
zip (zipper)	der Reißverschluß	derr righsfehrshluss

Electrical appliances and accessories—Records

220 volts, 50-cycle AC is almost universal in Germany as well as in Austria and Switzerland. Nevertheless, check the voltage before you plug your appliance in. You'll find an adaptor useful since the round pins on continental plugs are different from ours.

What's the voltage?	**Welche Spannung haben Sie hier?**	vehlkher shpahnung harbern zee heer
Is it AC or DC?	**Ist es Wechselstrom oder Gleichstrom?**	ist ehss vehkserlshtroam oaderr glighkhshtroam
Do you have a battery for...?	**Haben Sie eine Batterie für...?**	harbern zee ighner bahtehree fewr
Can you repair that?	**Können Sie das reparieren?**	kurnern zee dahss rehpahreerern
When will it be ready?	**Wann ist es fertig?**	vahn ist ehss fehrtik
I'd like a/an/some...	**Ich möchte...**	ikh murkhter
adaptor	**einen Zwischenstecker**	ighnern tsvishernshtehkerr
amplifier	**einen Verstärker**	ighnern fehrshtairkerr
battery	**eine Batterie**	ighner bahtehree
blender	**einen Mixer**	ighnern mikserr
clock	**eine Uhr**	ighner oor
wall clock	**Wanduhr**	vahntoor
food mixer	**einen Stabmixer**	ighnern shtarpmikserr
hair dryer	**einen Haartrockner**	ighnern harrtroknerr
iron	**ein Bügeleisen**	ighn bewgerlighzern
travelling iron	**Reisebügeleisen**	righzerbewgerlighzern
kettle	**einen Wassertopf**	ighnern vahssserrtopf
percolator	**eine Kaffeemaschine**	ighner kahfaymahsheener
plug	**einen Stecker**	ighnern shtehkerr
portable	**Koffer...**	kofferr
radio	**ein Radio**	ighn rardioa
car radio	**Autoradio**	owtoarardioa
record player	**einen Plattenspieler**	ighnern plahternshpeelerr
shaver	**einen Rasierapparat**	ighnern rahzeerahpahrart
speakers	**Lautsprecher**	lowtshprehkherr
tape recorder	**ein Tonbandgerät**	ighn toanbahntgerrait
cassette tape recorder	**einen Kassettenrekorder**	ighnern kahssehternrehkorderr

television	**einen Fernseher**	ighnern fehrnzayerr
colour television	**Farbfernseher**	fahrpfehrnzayerr
toaster	**einen Toaster**	ighnern toaster
transformer	**einen Transformator**	ighnern trahnsformartoar

Record shop

Do you have any records by...?	**Haben Sie Platten von...?**	harbern zee plahtern fon
Do you have...'s latest album?	**Haben Sie das neuste Album von...?**	harbern zee dahss noyster ahlbum fon
Can I listen to this record?	**Kann ich diese Platte hören?**	kahn ikh deezer plahter hurrern
I'd like a cassette.	**Ich hätte gern eine Kassette.**	ikh hehter gehrn ighner kahssehter
I want a new needle.	**Ich möchte eine neue Nadel.**	ikh murkhter ighner noyer narderl

L.P.	**die Langspielplatte**	dee lahngshpeelplahter
45 rpm	**fünfundvierzig UpM**	fewnfuntfeertsikh oo pay ehm
33 rpm	**dreiunddreißig UpM**	drighuntdrighssikh oo pay ehm

chamber music	**die Kammermusik**	dee kahmerrmuzeek
classical music	**die klassische Musik**	dee klahssisher muzeek
folk music	**die Volksmusik**	dee folksmuzeek
instrumental music	**die Instrumental-musik**	dee instrumehntarlmuzeek
jazz	**der Jazz**	derr dzhaiss
light music	**die Unterhaltungs-musik**	dee unterrhahltungsmuzeek
orchestral music	**die Orchestermusik**	dee orkehsterrmuzeek
pop music	**die Pop-Musik**	dee popmuzeek
yodelling music	**die Jodelmusik**	dee yoaderlmuzeek

Hairdressing—Barber's

I don't speak much German.	**Ich spreche nicht viel Deutsch.**	ikh **shprehkher** nikht feel doych
I want a haircut, please.	**Haare schneiden, bitte.**	harrer **shnighdern** bitter
I'd like a shave.	**Rasieren, bitte.**	rahzeerern bitter
Don't cut it too short.	**Nicht zu kurz.**	nikht tsu koorts
Scissors only, please.	**Nur mit der Schere, bitte.**	noor mit derr **shayrer** bitter
A razor cut, please.	**Einen Messer- schnitt, bitte.**	**ighnern** mehsserrshnit bitter
Don't use the clippers.	**Bitte keine Maschine.**	bitter **kighner** mahsheener
Just a trim, please.	**Nur ausputzen, bitte.**	noor owsputsern bitter
That's enough off.	**Das genügt.**	dahss **gernewgt**
A little more off the...	**Nehmen Sie...ein bißchen mehr weg.**	naymern zee ... **ighn** biskhern mayr vehk
back	**hinten**	hintern
neck	**im Nacken**	im **nahkern**
sides	**an den Seiten**	ahn dayn **zightern**
top	**oben**	**oabern**
I don't want any cream.	**Ich möchte keine Creme.**	ikh **murkhter kighner** kraym
Would you please trim my...?	**Stutzen Sie mir bitte...**	**shtutsern** zee meer bitter
beard	**den Bart**	dayn barrt
moustache	**den Schnurrbart**	dayn **shnoorbarrt**
sideboards (sideburns)	**die Koteletten**	dee **kotlehtern**
Thank you. That's fine.	**Sehr gut, danke.**	zayr goot **dahngker**
How much do I owe you?	**Was schulde ich Ihnen?**	vahss **shulder** ikh **eenern**
This is for you.	**Das ist für Sie.**	dahss ist fewr zee

FOR TIPPING, see inside back-cover

Ladies' hairdressing

Is there a hairdresser's in the hotel?	**Gibt es einen Damensalon im Hotel?**	gipt ehss **ighnern darmernzahlong** im hoatehl
Can I make an appointment for sometime on Thursday?	**Kann ich mich für Donnerstag anmelden?**	kahn ikh mikh fewr **donnerrstarg ahnmehldern**
I'd like it cut and shaped.	**Schneiden und Legen, bitte.**	**shnighdern** unt **laygern bitter**

with a fringe (bangs)	**Ponyfrisur**	poanifreezoor
page-boy style	**Pagenschnitt**	parzhernshnit
a razor cut	**ein Messerschnitt**	ighn **mehsserrshnit**
a re-style	**eine neue Frisur**	**ighner noyer** freezoor
with ringlets	**mit Löckchen**	mit lurkkhern
with waves	**mit Wellen**	mit vehlern
in a bun	**im Knoten**	im knoatern

I want a...	**Bitte...**	bitter
bleach	**eine Aufhellung**	**ighner** owfhehlung
colour rinse	**eine Farbspülung**	**ighner** fahrpshpewlung
dye	**eine Färbung**	**ighner** fairbung
permanent	**eine Dauerwelle**	**ighner** dowerrvehler
shampoo and set	**Waschen und Legen**	vahshern unt laygern
tint	**eine Tönung**	**ighner** turnung
touch up	**eine Auffrischung**	**ighner** owffrishung
the same colour	**dieselbe Farbe**	deezehlber fahrber
a darker colour	**eine dunklere Farbe**	**ighner** dungklerrer fahrber
a lighter colour	**eine hellere Farbe**	**ighner** hehlerrer fahrber
auburn/blond/ brunette	**kastanienbraun/ blond/braun**	kahstarniernbrown/blont/ brown
Do you have a colour chart?	**Haben Sie eine Farbtabelle?**	harbern zee **ighner** fahrptahbehler
I don't want any hairspray.	**Kein Haarspray, bitte.**	kighn harrshpray bitter
I want a...	**Ich möchte eine...**	ikh murkhter **ighner**
manicure/pedicure	**Maniküre/Pediküre**	mahnikkewrer,/ pehdikkewrer
face-pack	**Gesichtsmaske**	gerzikhtsmahsker

FOR TIPPING, see inside back-cover

Jeweller's—Watchmaker's

Can you repair this watch?	**Können Sie diese Uhr reparieren?**	kurnern zee deezer oor rehpahreerern
The...is broken.	**...ist kaputt.**	...ist kahput
glass / spring	**das Glas/die Feder**	dahss glahss/dee fayderr
strap	**das Armband**	dahss ahrmbahnt
winder	**der Kronenaufzug**	derr kroanernowftsoog
I want this watch cleaned.	**Ich möchte diese Uhr reinigen lassen.**	ikh murkhter deezer oor righniggern lahssern
When will it be ready?	**Wann ist sie fertig?**	vahn ist zee fehrtikh
Could I please see that?	**Könnte ich das bitte sehen?**	kurnter ikh dahss bitter zayern
I'm just looking around.	**Ich sehe mich nur um.**	ikh zayer mikh noor um
I want a small present for...	**Ich möchte ein kleines Geschenk für...**	ikh murkhter ighn klighnerss gershehngk fewr
I don't want anything too expensive.	**Ich möchte nichts zu Teures.**	ikh murkhter nikhts tsu toyrerss
I want something...	**Ich möchte etwas...**	ikh murkhter ehtvahss
better/cheaper	**Besseres/Billigeres**	behsserrerss/billigerrerss
simpler	**Einfacheres**	ighnfahkherrerss
Is this real silver?	**Ist das echt Silber?**	ist dahss ehkt zilberr
Do you have anything in gold?	**Haben Sie etwas in Gold?**	harbern zee ehtvahss in golt

If it's made of gold, ask:

How many carats is this?	**Wieviel Karat hat es?**	veefeel kahrart haht ehss

When you go to a jeweller's, you've probably got some idea of what you want beforehand. Find out what the article is made of and then look up the name of the article itself in the following lists.

SHOPPING GUIDE

What's it made of?

amber	Bernstein	behrnshtighn
amethyst	Amethyst	ahmehtist
chromium	Chrom	kroam
copper	Kupfer	kupferr
coral	Koralle	korrahler
crystal	Kristall	kristahl
cut glass	geschliffenes Glas	gershliffernerss glahss
diamond	Diamant	diahmahnt
ebony	Ebenholz	aybernholts
emerald	Smaragd	smahrahgt
enamel	Email	ehmahi
glass	Glas	glahss
gold	Gold	golt
gold plate	vergoldet	fehrgoldert
ivory	Elfenbein	ehlfernbighn
jade	Jade	yarder
onyx	Onyx	oaniks
pearl	Perle	pehrler
pewter	Zinn	tsin
platinum	Platin	plarteen
ruby	Rubin	rubeen
sapphire	Saphir	zahfeer
silver	Silber	zilberr
silver plate	versilbert	fehrzilbert
stainless steel	rostfreier Stahl	rostfrigherr shtarl
topaz	Topas	topparss
turquoise	Türkis	tewrkeess

What is it?

I'd like a/an/some...	Ich möchte...	ikh murkhter
bangle	einen Reif	ighnern righf
beads	eine Perlenschnur	ighner pehrlernshnoor
bracelet	ein Armband	ighn ahrmbahnt
charm bracelet	Amulettarmband	ahmullehtahrmbahnt
brooch	eine Brosche	ighner brosher
chain	ein Kettchen	ighn kehtkhern
charm	ein Amulett	ighn ahmulleht
cigarette case	ein Zigarettenetui	ighn tsiggahrehternehtvee
cigarette lighter	ein Feuerzeug	ighn foyerrtsoyg
clock	eine Uhr	ighner oor
alarm clock	einen Wecker	ighnern vehkerr
cuckoo clock	eine Kuckucksuhr	ighner kukkuksoor

travelling clock	einen Reisewecker	ighnern righzervehkerr
wall clock	eine Wanduhr	ighner vahndoor
collar stud	einen Kragenknopf	ighnern krargernknopf
cross	ein Kreuz	ighn kroyts
cuff-links	Manschettenknöpfe	mahnshehternknurpfer
earrings	Ohrringe	oarringer
jewel box	ein Schmuck-kästchen	ighn shmuk-kehstkhern
manicure set	ein Maniküreetui	ighn mahnikkewrehtvee
mechanical pencil	einen Drehbleistift	ighnern drayblighshtift
necklace	eine Halskette	ighner hahlskehter
pendant	einen Anhänger	ighnern ahnhehngerr
pin	eine Anstecknadel	ighner ahnstehknarderl
powder compact	eine Puderdose	ighner pooderrdoazer
propelling pencil	einen Drehbleistift	ighnern drayblighshtift
ring	einen Ring	ighnern ring
engagement ring	Verlobungsring	fehrloabungsring
signet ring	Siegelring	zeegerlring
wedding ring	Ehering	ayerring
rosary	einen Rosenkranz	ighnern roazernkrahnts
silver plate (silverware)	Tafelsilber	tarferlzilberr
snuff box	eine Schnupftabak-dose	ighner shnupftahbahk-doazer
strap	ein Armband	ighn ahrmbahnt
chain strap	Gliederarmband	gleederrahrmbahnt
leather strap	Lederarmband	layderrahrmbahnt
tie clip	einen Krawatten-klipp	ighnern krahvahternklip
tie pin	eine Krawatten-nadel	ighner krahvahternnarderl
vanity case	ein Ziertäschchen	ighn tseertehshkhern
watch	eine Uhr	ighner oor
pocket watch	Taschenuhr	tahshernoor
with a second hand	mit Sekundenzeiger	mit zehkunderntsighgerr
wristwatch	Armbanduhr	ahrmbahntoor

Laundry—Dry cleaning

If your hotel doesn't have its own laundry or dry cleaning service, ask the porter:

Where's the nearest laundry/dry cleaner's?	**Wo ist die nächste Wäscherei/chemische Reinigung?**	voa ist dee **nehkh**ster vehsherrigh/**khay**misher righnigung
I want these clothes...	**Ich möchte diese Kleider... lassen.**	ikh **murkh**ter **dee**zer **kligh**derr ... **lahs**sern
cleaned	**reinigen**	**righ**niggern
ironed	**bügeln**	**bewg**erln
pressed	**dampfbügeln**	**dahmpf**bewgerln
washed	**waschen**	**vahsh**ern
When will it be ready?	**Wann ist es fertig?**	vahn ist ehss **fehr**tikh
I need it...	**Ich brauche es...**	ikh **browkh**er ehss
today	**heute**	**hoy**ter
tonight	**heute abend**	**hoy**ter **ar**behrnt
tomorrow	**morgen**	**morg**ern
before Friday	**vor Freitag**	foar **frigh**targ
I want it as soon as possible.	**Ich möchte es so schnell wie möglich.**	ikh **murkh**ter ehss zoa shnehl vee **murg**likh
Can you...this?	**Können Sie das...?**	**kurn**ern zee dahss
mend	**ausbessern**	**ows**behssern
patch	**flicken**	**flik**kern
stitch	**nähen**	**nai**ern
Can you sew on this button?	**Können Sie diesen Knopf annähen?**	**kurn**ern zee **dee**zern knopf **ahn**naiern
Can you get this stain out?	**Können Sie diesen Fleck entfernen?**	**kurn**ern zee **dee**zern flehk **ehnt**fehrnern
Can this be invisibly mended?	**Können Sie das kunststopfen?**	**kurn**ern zee dahss **kunst**shtopfern
Is my laundry ready?	**Ist meine Wäsche fertig?**	ist **migh**ner **veh**sher **fehr**tikh
This isn't mine.	**Das gehört nicht mir.**	dahss ger**hurrt** nikht meer
There's one piece missing.	**Es fehlt ein Stück.**	ehss faylt ighn shtewk
There's a hole in this.	**Da ist ein Loch drin.**	dar ist ighn lokh drin

Photography

I want an inexpensive camera.	Ich möchte eine preiswerte Kamera.	ikh **murkhter** **ighner** **prighs**vayter **kah**mehrar
Show me that one in the window.	Zeigen Sie mir die aus dem Schaufenster.	**tsigh**ern zee meer dee owss daym **show**fehnsterr

Film

Film sizes aren't always indicated the same way on the Continent as in the U.S.A. and Great Britain. Listed below you'll find some equivalents and translations which will be useful.

I'd like a...	Ich hätte gern...	ikh **hehter** gehrn
film for this camera	einen Film für diese Kamera	**ighnern** film fewr **deezer** **kah**mehrar
120	sechs mal sechs (6×6)	zehks marl zehks
127	vier mal vier (4×4)	feer marl feer
135	vierundzwanzig mal sechsunddreißig (24×36)	**feer**unttsvahntsikh marl **zehks**untdrighssikh
8-mm film	einen acht Millimeter Film	**ighnern** ahkht **milli**mayterr film
regular	Einfach acht	**ighn**fahkh ahkht
double 8	Doppel acht	**dopperl** ahkht
super 8	Super acht	**zooperr** ahkht
16-mm film	einen sechzehn Millimeter Film	**ighnern** **zehkht**sayn **milli**mayterr film
20 exposures	zwanzig Aufnahmen	**tsvahntsikh** **owf**narmern
36 exposures	sechsunddreißig Aufnahmen	**zehks**untdrighssikh **owf**narmern
this ASA/DIN number	diese ASA/DIN Zahl	**deezer** arzar/deen tsarl
fast	höchstempfindlich	**hurkhst**ehmpfindlikh
fine grain	Feinkorn	**fighn**korn
black and white	schwarzweiß	**shvahrts**vighss
colour	Farbfilm	**fahrp**film
colour negative	Farbnegativ	**fahrp**nehgahteef
colour slide	Farbdiapositive	**fahrp**deeahpoazitteever
artificial light type	Kunstlichtfilm	**kunst**likhtfilm
daylight type	Tageslichtfilm	**targers**likhtfilm
Does the price include developing?	Ist das Entwickeln im Preis inbegriffen?	ist dahss ehntvikkerln im **prighss** inbergriffern

FOR NUMBERS, see page 175

Processing

How much do you charge for developing?	Was kostet das Entwickeln?	vahss kostert dahss ehntvikkerln
I want...prints of each negative.	Ich möchte... Abzüge von jedem Negativ.	ikh murkhter ... ahpzewger fon yayderm nehgahteef
with a mat finish	matt	maht
with a glossy finish	Hochglanz	hokhglahnts
Will you please enlarge this?	Können Sie das bitte vergrößern?	kurnern zee dahss bitter fehrgrursserrn
When will it be ready?	Wann ist es fertig?	vahn ist ehss fehrtikh

Accessories and repairs

I want a/some...	Ich möchte...	ikh murkhter
flash bulbs	Blitzlampen	blitslahmpern
flash cubes	Blitzwürfel	blitsvewrferl
for black and white	für schwarzweiß	fewr shvahrtsvighss
for colour	für Farbe	fewr fahrber
lens cap	einen Objektivdeckel	ighnern obyehkteefdehkerl
lens cleaners	Objektivreiniger	obyehkteefrighnigerr
red filter	einen Rotfilter	ighnern roatfilterr
yellow filter	einen Gelbfilter	ighnern gehlpfilterr
ultra-violet filter	einen Ultraviolett-filter	ighnern ultrahvioaleht-filterr
Can you repair this camera?	Können Sie diese Kamera reparieren?	kurnern zee deezer kahmehrar rehpahreerern
The film is jammed.	Der Film klemmt.	dehr film klehmt
There's something wrong with the...	Mit...stimmt etwas nicht.	mit ... shtimt ehtvahss nikht
exposure counter	dem Bildzählwerk	daym bilttsailvehrk
film winder	dem Transportknopf	daym trahnsportknopf
flash contact	dem Blitzkontakt	daym blitskontahkt
lens	dem Objektiv	daym obyehkteef
light meter	dem Belichtungs-messer	daym berlikhtungsmehsserr
rangefinder	dem Entfernungs-messer	daym ehntfehrnungsmehss
shutter	dem Verschluß	daym fehrshluss

Provisions

Here's a basic list of food and drink that you might want on a picnic or for the occasional meal at home:

I'd like some..., please. **Ich möchte bitte...** ikh murkhter bitter

apple juice	**Apfelsaft**	ahpferlzahft
apples	**Äpfel**	ehpferl
bananas	**Bananen**	bahnarnern
biscuits (Br.)	**Kekse**	kaykser
bread	**Brot**	broat
butter	**Butter**	butterr
cake	**Kuchen**	kookhern
candy	**Konfekt**	konfehkt
cheese	**Käse**	kaizer
chocolate	**Schokolade**	shokkollarder
coffee	**Kaffee**	kahfay
cold cuts	**Aufschnitt**	owfshnit
cookies	**Kekse**	kaykser
cooking fat	**Kochfett**	kokhfeht
crackers	**Cräckers**	krehkerr
crisps	**Kartoffelchips**	kahrtofferlchips
cucumbers	**Gurken**	goorkern
eggs	**Eier**	igherr
flour	**Mehl**	mayl
frankfurters	**Frankfurter Würstchen**	frahnkfoorterr vewrstkhern
grapefruit juice	**Pampelmusensaft**	pahmperlmoozernzahft
grapefruits	**Pampelmusen**	pahmperlmoozern
ham	**Schinken**	shingkern
ice-cream	**Eis**	ighss
lemons	**Zitronen**	tsitroanern
lettuce	**Kopfsalat**	kopfzahlart
liver sausage	**Leberwurst**	layberrvoorst
milk	**Milch**	milkh
mustard	**Senf**	zehnf
oil	**Öl**	url
orange juice	**Apfelsinensaft**	ahpferlzeenernzahft
oranges	**Apfelsinen**	ahpferlzeenern
pepper	**Pfeffer**	pfehferr
pickles	**Essiggemüse**	ehssikhgermewzer
potato chips	**Kartoffelchips**	kahrtofferlchips
potatoes	**Kartoffeln**	kahrtofferln
rolls	**Brötchen**	brurtkhern
salad	**Salat**	zahlart

salami	**Salami**	zahlarmee
salt	**Salz**	zahlts
sandwiches	**Sandwichs**	**zehnt**vichs
sausages	**Würstchen**	vewrstkhern
spaghetti	**Spaghetti**	spah**geh**tee
sugar	**Zucker**	tsukkerr
sweets	**Konfekt**	kon**fehkt**
tea	**Tee**	tay
tomato juice	**Tomatensaft**	tommarternzahft
tomatoes	**Tomaten**	tom**martern**
yoghurt	**Joghurt**	**yoa**goort

And don't forget…

a bottle opener	**einen Flaschenöffner**	**igh**nern **flahsh**ernurfnerr
a corkscrew	**einen Korkenzieher**	**igh**nern korkerntseeherr
matches	**Streichhölzer**	**shtrigh**khhurltserr
paper napkins	**Papierservietten**	pah**peer**zehrviehtern
a tin (can) opener	**einen Büchsenöffner**	**igh**nern **bewk**sernurfnerr

---

Weights and measures

1 kilogram or kilo (kg) = 1000 grams (g)

| 100 g = 3.5 oz. | ½ kg = 1.1 lb. |
| 200 g = 7.0 oz. | 1 kg = 2.2 lb. |

1 oz. = 28.35 g
1 lb. = 453.60 g

---

1 litre (l) = 0.88 imp. quarts = 1.06 U.S. quarts

| 1 imp. quart = 1.14 l | 1 U.S. quart = 0.95 l |
| 1 imp. gallon = 4.55 l | 1 U.S. gallon = 3.8 l |

---

bottle	**die Flasche**	dee **flah**sher
box	**die Schachtel**	dee **shahkh**terl
can	**die Büchse/Dose**	dee **bewk**ser/**doa**zer
carton	**die Packung**	dee **pah**kung
crate	**die Kiste**	dee **kis**ter
jar	**das Glas**	dahss glahss
packet	**die Packung**	dee **pah**kung
tin	**die Büchse/Dose**	dee **bewk**ser/**doa**zer
tube	**die Tube**	dee **too**ber

Souvenirs

Here are some suggestions for articles which you may wish to buy as gifts or souvenirs when in Germany:

Bavarian peasant dress	das Dirndl (Kleid)	dahss deerndl(klight)
beer stein	der Bierkrug	derr beerkroog
camera	die Kamera	dee kahmehrar
cutlery	das Tafelbesteck	dahss tarferlbershtehk
doll	die Puppe	dee pupper
glassware	die Glaswaren	dee glahsvarrern
leather goods	die Lederwaren	dee layderrvarrern
music box	die Spieldose	dee shpeeldoazer
porcelain	das Porzellan	dahss portsehlarn
silver plate (silverware)	das Tafelsilber	dahss tarferlzilberr
toy	das Spielzeug	dahss shpeeltsoyg
waterproof woollen overcoat	der Lodenmantel	derr loadernmahnterl
wood carving	die Holzschnitzarbeit	dee holtsshnitsahrbight

Remember to find out whether you're entitled to reimbursement of value-added tax *(Mehrwertsteuer)* for the article you bought.

The high quality of Austrian and Swiss winter sports equipment is well known. But petit-point embroidery and porcelain in Austria and linens and organdies in Switzerland easily catch the feminine eye. Look into leather goods and *Lederhosen* (knee-length leather trousers) in Austria while not missing the fabulous array of watches and luscious chocolate in Switzerland.

chocolate	die Schokolade	dee shokkollarder
cuckoo clock	die Kuckucksuhr	dee kukkuksoor
embroidery	die Stickerei	dee shtikkerrigh
linen	das Leinenzeug	dahss lighnerntsoyg
ski equipment	die Schiausrüstung	dee sheeowsrewstung
Tyrolean hat	der Tirolerhut	derr teeroalerrhoot
Tyrolean pipe	die Tiroler Pfeife	dee teeroalerr pfighfer
watch	die Uhr	dee oor

Tobacconist's

As at home, cigarettes are generally referred to by their brand names, e.g., *Ernte* (**ehrn**ter), *HB* (har **bay**) and *Rothändle* (**roat**hehndler).

Give me a / an / some..., please.	Geben Sie mir bitte...	gaybern zee meer bitter
ashtray	einen Aschenbecher	ighnern ahshernbehkherr
chewing tobacco	Kautabak	kowtahbahk
cigar	eine Zigarre	ighner tsiggahrer
cigars	ein paar Zigarren	ighn parr tsiggahrern
cigarette case	ein Zigarettenetui	ighn tsiggahrehternehtvee
cigarette holder	eine Zigaretten-spitze	ighner tsiggahrehtern-shpitser
cigarette lighter	ein Feuerzeug	ighn foyerrtsoyg
flints	Feuersteine	foyerrshtighner
humidor	einen Tabaktopf	ighnern tahbahktopf
lighter fluid	Feuerzeugbenzin	foyerrtsoygbehntseen
lighter gas	Feuerzeuggas	foyerrtsoyggarss
matches	Streichhölzer	shtrighkhhurltserr
packet of cigarettes	eine Schachtel Zigaretten	ighner shahkhterl tsiggahrèhtern
packet of...	eine Schachtel...	ighner shahkhterl
pipe	eine Pfeife	ighner pfighfer
pipe cleaners	Pfeifenreiniger	pfighfernrighniggerr
pipe rack	einen Pfeifen-ständer	ighnern pfighfern-shtehnderr
pipe tobacco	Pfeifentabak	pfighferntahbahk
pipe tool	ein Pfeifenbesteck	ighn pfighfernbehshtehk
snuff	Schnupftabak	shnupftahbahk
tobacco pouch	einen Tabakbeutel	ighnern tahbahkboyterl
wick	einen Docht	ighnern dokht
Do you have any...?	Haben Sie...?	harbern zee
American cigarettes	amerikanische Zigaretten	ahmehrikarnisher tsiggahrehtern
English cigarettes	englische Zigaretten	ehnglisher tsiggahrehtern
menthol cigarettes	Mentholzigaretten	mehntoaltsiggahrehtern

filter tipped	mit Filter	mit filterr
without filter	ohne Filter	oaner filterr
king-size	extra lang	ehkstrar lahng

| I'll take two packets. | **Ich nehme zwei Schachteln.** | ikh **nay**mer tsvigh **shahkh**terln |
| I'd like a carton. | **Ich möchte eine Stange.** | ikh **murkh**ter **igh**ner **shtah**nger |

While we're on the subject of cigarettes, suppose you want to offer somebody one?

Would you like a cigarette?	**Darf ich Ihnen eine Zigarette anbieten?**	dahrf ikh **ee**nern **igh**ner tsiggah**reh**ter **ahn**beetern
Have one of mine.	**Nehmen Sie eine von meinen.**	**nay**mern zee **igh**ner fon **migh**nern
Try one of these.	**Versuchen Sie mal eine von diesen.**	fehr**zoo**khern zee marl **igh**ner fon **dee**zern
They're very mild.	**Sie sind sehr mild.**	zee zint zayr milt
They're a bit strong.	**Sie sind ziemlich stark.**	zee zint **tseem**likh shtahrk

And if somebody offers you one?

Thank you.	**Danke.**	**dahng**ker
No, thanks.	**Nein danke.**	nighn **dahng**ker
I don't smoke.	**Ich rauche nicht.**	ikh **row**kher nikht
I've given it up.	**Ich rauche nicht mehr.**	ikh **row**kher nikht mayr

Your money: banks—currency

Banking hours in Germany are usually from 8.30 a.m. to 12.30 p.m. and from 1.30 to 4 p.m., Monday to Friday (Thursday until 5.30 p.m.). Hours are slightly different in Austria and Switzerland.

The *Deutsche Mark* (abbreviated to *DM* and called *D-Mark*—**day** mahrk) is the unit of currency in Germany. It's divided into 100 *Pfennig* (**pfeh**nikh). There are coins of 1 and 2 pfennigs (rare nowadays) and 5, 10 and 50 pfennigs and of 1, 2 and 5 marks. Banknotes: 5, 10, 20, 50, 100, 500 and 1000 marks.

In Austria, the basic unit is the *Schilling* (**shil**ling), abbreviated *S*. It's divided into 100 *Groschen* (**gro**shern), abbreviated *g*. Coin denominations are as follows: 2, 5, 10 and 50 groschen and 1, 5, 10 and 25 schillings. There are banknotes of 20, 50, 100, 500 and 1000 schillings.

The *Franken* (**frahng**kern), usually abbreviated *Fr.,* is the Swiss unit of currency. There are 100 *Rappen* (**rah**pern), abbreviated *Rp.,* to a franc. Coins are of 5, 10, 20 and 50 Rappen and 1, 2 and 5 franc denominations. Banknotes: 10, 20, 50, 100, 500 and 1000 francs.

In Germany, as well as in Austria and Switzerland, you'll find numerous small currency-exchange offices, indicated by the words *Geldwechsel* or *Wechselstube.* Sometimes they're open outside regular banking hours.

Where's the nearest bank?	**Wo ist die nächste Bank?**	voa ist dee **nehkh**ster bahngk
Where can I find a currency-exchange office?	**Wo finde ich eine Wechselstube?**	voa **fin**der ikh **igh**ner **vehks**erlshtoober
Where can I cash a traveller's cheque (check)?	**Wo kann ich einen Reisescheck einlösen?**	voa kahn ikh **igh**nern **righz**ershehk **ighn**lurzern

Inside

I want to change some dollars.	Ich möchte einige Dollar wechseln.	ikh murkhter ighnigger dollar vehkserln
I'd like to change some pounds.	Ich möchte einige Pfund wechseln.	ikh murkhter ighnigger pfunt vehkserln
Here's my passport.	Hier ist mein Paß.	heer ist mighn pahss
What's the exchange rate?	Wie ist der Wechselkurs?	vee ist derr vehkserlkoorss
What rate of commission do you charge?	Welche Gebühr erheben Sie?	wehlkher gerbewr ehrhaybern zee
Can you cash a personal cheque?	Können Sie einen Barscheck einlösen?	kurnern zee ighnern barrshehk ighnlurzern
How long will it take to clear?	Wie lange brauchen Sie für die Überprüfung?	vee lahnger browkhern zee fewr dee ewberrprewfung
Can you wire my bank in London?	Können Sie meiner Bank in London telegraphieren?	kurnern zee mighnerr bahngk in london taylaygrahfeerern
I have...	Ich habe...	ikh harber
a letter of credit	einen Kreditbrief	ighnern krayditbreef
an introduction from...	einen Empfehlungsbrief von...	ighnern ehmpfaylungsbreef fon
a credit card	eine Kreditkarte	ighner krayditkahrter
I'm expecting some money from Boston. Has it arrived yet?	Ich erwarte Geld aus Boston. Ist es schon angekommen?	ikh ehrvahrter gehlt owss boston. ist ehss shoan ahngerkommern
Please give me... notes (bills) and some small change.	Geben Sie mir bitte... Scheine und etwas Kleingeld.	gaybern zee meer bitter ... shighner unt ehtvahss klighngehlt
Give me...large notes and the rest in small notes.	Geben Sie mir... große Scheine und den Rest in kleinen Scheinen.	gaybern zee meer ... groasser shighner unt dayn rehst in klighnern shighnern
Could you please check that again?	Könnten Sie das bitte nochmal nachrechnen?	kurntern zee dahss bitter nokhmarl nahkhrehkhnern

Depositing

I want to credit this to my account.	**Ich möchte das auf mein Konto einzahlen.**	ikh murkhter dahss owf mighn kontoa ighntsarlerr
I want to credit this to Mr...'s account.	**Ich möchte dies auf das Konto von Herrn... einzahlen.**	ikh murkhter deess owf dahss kontoa fon hehrn ... ighntsarlern
Where should I sign?	**Wo muß ich unterschreiben?**	voa muss ikh unterrshrighbern

Currency converter

In a world of floating currencies, we can offer no more than this do-it-yourself chart. You can get a card showing current exchange rates from banks, travel agents and tourist offices. Why not fill in this chart, too, for handy reference?

	£	$
1 German mark		
5		
20		
50		
100		
1 Austrian shilling		
5		
20		
50		
100		
1 Swiss franc		
5		
20		
50		
100		

At the post-office

The offices of Germany's *Bundespost* are open from 8 a.m. to midday and from 2 to 6.30 p.m. They close at noon on Saturdays. Mail-boxes in Germany are painted yellow. Swiss post-offices are open from 7.30 a.m. to midday and from 1.30 to 6.30 p.m. (8 to 11 a.m. on Saturdays). Mail-boxes are yellow. In Austria, post-offices are open from 8 a.m. to midday and from 2 to 5 p.m. (8 to 10 a.m. on Saturdays). Austrian mail-boxes are yellow or blue.

In principal cities, some post-offices are open outside the normal hours. Remember that for telephoning and cables you should go to the post-office—there are no separate telephone or cable offices.

Where's the nearest post-office?	**Wo ist das nächste Postamt?**	voa ist dahss **nehkhster postahmt**
What time does the post-office open/close?	**Wann wird das Postamt geöffnet/geschlossen?**	vahn veert dahss **postahmt** gerurfnert/gershlossern
What window do I go to for stamps?	**An welchem Schalter gibt es Briefmarken?**	ahn **vehlkherm shahlterr** gipt ehss **breefmahrkern**
At which counter can I cash an international money order?	**An welchem Schalter kann ich eine internationale Postanweisung einlösen?**	ahn **vehlkherm shahlterr** kahn ikh **ighner** interrnahtsioanarler postahnvighzung **ighnlurzern**
I want...40-pfennig stamps.	**Ich möchte... Briefmarken zu 40 Pfennig.**	ikh **murkhter...** breefmahrkern tsu 40 pfehnikh
What's the postage for a letter/a postcard to London?	**Was kostet ein Brief/eine Postkarte nach London?**	vahss kostert ighn breef/ighner postkahrter nahkh london
Do I need to fill in a customs declaration?	**Muß ich ein Zollerklärungs-formular ausfüllen?**	muss ikh ighn **tsoll**-ehrklairungsformullarr owsfewlern

POST OFFICE

Do all letters go airmail?	Gehen alle Briefe per Luftpost?	gayern ahler breefer pehr luftpost
I want to send this parcel.	Ich möchte ein Paket aufgeben.	ikh murkhter ighn pahkayt owfgaybern
Where's the mailbox?	Wo ist der Briefkasten?	voa ist derr breefkahstern
I want to send this by...	Ich möchte dies... senden.	ikh murkhter deess... zehndern
airmail	per Luftpost	pehr luftpost
express (special delivery)	per Eilboten	pehr ighlboatern
registered mail	eingeschrieben	ighngershreebern
Where's the poste restante (general delivery)?	Wo ist der Schalter für postlagernde Sendungen?	voa ist derr shahlterr fewr postlargerrnder zehndungern
Is there any mail for me? My name is...	Ist Post für mich da? Ich heiße...	ist post fewr mikh dar? ikh highsser

BRIEFMARKEN	STAMPS
PAKETE	PARCELS
POSTANWEISUNGEN	MONEY ORDERS

Cables (telegrams)

I want to send a telegram. May I please have a form?	Ich möchte ein Telegramm aufgeben. Kann ich bitte ein Formular haben?	ikh murkhter ighn taylaygrahm owfgaybern. kahn ikh bitter ighn formullarr harbern
How much is it per word?	Was kostet es pro Wort?	vahss kostert ehss proa vort
How long will a cable to Chicago take?	Wie lange braucht ein Telegramm nach Chicago?	vee lahnger browkht ighn taylaygrahm nahkh tshikkargoa
I'd like to send a night-letter.	Ich möchte ein Brieftelegramm aufgeben.	ikh murkhter ighn breeftaylaygrahm owfgaybern

Telephoning

The telephone networks of Germany, Austria and Switzerland are almost entirely automated. Coin-operated booths are to be found on the street, with instructions posted inside, often in English.

In Germany, international calls can be made from special booths marked with a green disc and the sign *Ausland*. They can be made from almost all public telephones in Switzerland. In Austria, only some are equipped for long-distance calls.

Phone numbers are given in pairs. Note that, in telephoning, *zwei* becomes *zwo* (tsvoa).

Where's the telephone?	**Wo ist das Telephon?**	voa ist dahss taylay**foan**
Where's the nearest telephone booth?	**Wo ist die nächste Telephonzelle?**	voa ist dee **nehkh**ster taylay**foan**tsehler
May I use your phone?	**Darf ich Ihr Telephon benutzen?**	dahrf ikh eer taylay**foan** bernutsern
Do you have a telephone directory for Bonn?	**Haben Sie ein Telephonbuch von Bonn?**	harbern zee ighn taylay**foan**bukh fon bon
Can you help me get this number?	**Können Sie mir helfen, diese Nummer zu bekommen?**	kurnern zee meer **hehl**fern **deezer nummerr** tsu ber**kom**mern

Operator

Do you speak English?	**Sprechen Sie Englisch?**	shprehkhern zee **ehng**lish
Good morning, I want Hamburg 123456.	**Guten Morgen. Ich möchte Hamburg 123456.**	gootern morgern. ikh **murkh**ter hahmboorg 123456
Can I dial direct?	**Kann ich durchwählen?**	kahn ikh **doorkh**vailern
I want to place a personal (person-to-person) call.	**Ich möchte ein Gespräch mit Voranmeldung.**	ikh **murkh**ter ighn gershpraikh mit **foar**ahnmehldung

FOR NUMBERS, see page 175

| I want to reverse the charges. | Ich möchte ein R-Gespräch anmelden. | ikh murkhter ighn ehr-gershpraikh ahnmehldern |
| Will you tell me the cost of the call afterwards? | Würden Sie mir anschließend die Gebühr mitteilen? | vewrdern zee meer ahnshleessernt dee gerbewr mittighlern |

Telephone alphabet

A	Anton	ahntoan	O	Otto	ottoa
Ä	Ärger	ehrgerr	Ö	Ökonom	urkoanoam
B	Berta	behrtar	P	Paula	powlah
C	Caesar	tsaizahr	Q	Quelle	kvehler
CH	Charlotte	shahrlotter	R	Richard	rikhahrt
D	Dora	doarah	S	Samuel	zarmuehl
E	Emil	aymeel	SCH	Schule	shooler
F	Friedrich	freedrikh	T	Theodor	tayoadoar
G	Gustav	gustahf	U	Ulrich	ulrikh
H	Heinrich	highnrikh	Ü	Übel	ewberl
I	Ida	eedah	V	Viktor	viktoar
J	Julius	yooliuss	W	Wilhelm	vilhehlm
K	Kaufmann	kowfmahn	X	Xanthippe	ksahntipper
L	Ludwig	ludvig	Y	Ypsilon	ewpzeeloan
M	Martha	mahrtah	Z	Zacharias	tsahkhahreeahss
N	Nordpol	nortpoal			

Speaking

Hello. This is... speaking.	Hallo. Hier spricht...	hahloa. heer shprikht
I want to speak to...	Ich möchte... sprechen.	ikh murkhter shprehkhern
Would you put me through to...?	Verbinden Sie mich bitte mit...	fehrbindern zee mikh bitter mit
I want extension...	Ich möchte Nebenanschluß...	ikh murkhter naybern-ahnshluss
Is that...?	Ist dort...?	ist dort

Bad luck

| Would you please try again later? | Würden Sie es bitte später noch einmal versuchen? | vewrdern zee ehss bitter shpaiterr nokh ighnmarl fehrzookhern |

| Operator, you gave me the wrong number. | Fräulein, Sie haben mich falsch verbunden. | froylighn zee harbern mikh fahlsh fehrbundern |
| We were cut off. | Wir sind unterbrochen worden. | veer zint unterrbrokhern vordern |

Not there

When will he/she be back?	Wann kommt er/sie zurück?	vahn komt ehr/zee tsoorewk
Will you tell him/her I called? My name's...	Würden Sie ihm/ihr sagen, daß ich angerufen habe? Mein Name ist...	vewrdern zee eem/eer zargern dahss ikh ahngerroofern harber? mighn narmer ist
Would you ask him/her to call me?	Würden Sie ihn/sie bitten, mich anzurufen?	vewrdern zee een/zee bittern mikh ahntsooroofern
Would you please take a message?	Würden Sie bitte etwas ausrichten?	vewrdern zee bitter ehtvahss owsrikhtern

Charges

| What was the cost of that call? | Was hat das Gespräch gekostet? | vahss haht dahss gershpraikh gerkostert |
| I want to pay for the call. | Ich möchte das Gespräch bezahlen. | ikh murkhter dahss gershpraikh bertsarlern |

Ein Anruf für Sie.	There's a telephone call for you.
Welche Nummer haben Sie gewählt?	What number are you calling?
Die Linie ist besetzt.	The line's engaged.
Es meldet sich niemand.	There's no answer.
Sie sind falsch verbunden.	You've got the wrong number.
Das Telephon funktioniert nicht.	The phone is out of order.
Er/Sie ist im Augenblick nicht da.	He's/She's out at the moment.

The car

Filling station

We'll start this section by considering your possible needs at a filling station. Most of them don't handle major repairs; but apart from providing you with fuel, they may be helpful in solving all kinds of minor problems.

Where's the nearest filling station?	**Wo ist die nächste Tankstelle?**	voa ist dee nehkhster tahnkshtehler
I want 20 litres of petrol (gas), please.	**Ich möchte 20 Liter Benzin, bitte.**	ikh murkhter 20 leeterr behntseen bitter
I want 30 litres of standard/premium.	**Ich möchte 30 Liter Normal/Super.**	ikh murkhter 30 leeterr normarl/zooperr
Give me 25 marks worth of...	**Für 25 Mark...**	fewr 25 mahrk
Fill her up, please.	**Voll, bitte.**	fol bitter
Please check the oil and water.	**Kontrollieren Sie bitte Ölstand und Wasser.**	kontroleerern zee bitter urlshtahnt unt vahsserr
Give me 2 litres of oil.	**Geben Sie mir 2 Liter Öl.**	gaybern zee meer 2 leeterr url
Fill up the battery with distilled water.	**Füllen Sie bitte destilliertes Wasser in der Batterie nach.**	fewlern zee bitter dehstilleerterss vahsser in derr bahtehree nahkh
Check the brake fluid.	**Kontrollieren Sie die Bremsflüssigkeit.**	kontroleerern zee dee brehmsflewssikhkight

Fluid measures					
litres	imp. gal.	U.S. gal.	litres	imp. gal.	U.S. gal.
5	1.1	1.3	30	6.6	7.8
10	2.2	2.6	35	7.7	9.1
15	3.3	3.9	40	8.8	10.4
20	4.4	5.2	45	9.9	11.7
25	5.5	6.5	50	11.0	13.0

FOR NUMBERS, see page 175

| Would you check the tire pressure? | Würden Sie bitte den Reifendruck prüfen? | vewrdern zee bitter dayn righferndruk prewfern |
| .6 front, 1.8 rear. | Vorne 1,6, hinten 1,8.* | forner 1,6 hintern 1,8 |

Tire pressure			
lb./sq. in.	kg./cm²	lb./sq. in.	kg./cm²
10	0.7	26	1.8
12	0.8	27	1 9
15	1.1	28	2.0
18	1.3	30	2.1
20	1.4	33	2.3
21	1.5	36	2.5
23	1.6	38	2.7
24	1.7	40	2.8

Please check the spare tire, too.	Prüfen Sie auch den Ersatzreifen, bitte.	prewfern zee owkh dayn ehrzahtsrighfern bitter
Can you mend this puncture (fix this flat)?	Können Sie diesen Reifen flicken?	kurnern zee deezern righfern flikkern
Would you please change this tire?	Würden Sie bitte diesen Reifen wechseln?	vewrdern zee bitter deezern righfern vehkserln
Would you clean the windscreen (windshield)?	Würden Sie bitte die Windschutzscheibe reinigen?	vewrdern zee bitter dee vintshutsshighber righniggern
Have you a road map of this district?	Haben Sie eine Straßenkarte von dieser Gegend?	harbern zee ighner shtrarssernkahrter fon deezerr gaygernt
Where are the toilets?	Wo sind die Toiletten?	voa zint dee toaahlehtern

* Germans don't say, for instance, one *point* eight but simply one eight (*eins acht* – ighns ahkht) or one *comma* eight (*eins komma acht* – ighns kommah ahkht).

Asking the way—Street directions

Excuse me.	**Entschuldigung.**	ehntshuldiggung
Can you tell me the way to…?	**Können Sie mir sagen, wie ich nach… komme?**	kurnern zee meer zargern vee ikh nahkh …kommer
How do I get to…?	**Wie komme ich nach…?**	vee kommer ikh nahkh
Where does this road lead to?	**Wohin führt diese Straße?**	voahin fewrt deezer shtrahsser
Are we on the right road for…?	**Sind wir auf der richtigen Straße nach…?**	zint veer owf derr rikhtiggern shtrahsser nahkh
How far is the next village?	**Wie weit ist es bis zum nächsten Dorf?**	vee vight ist ehss biss tsum nehkhstern dorf
How far is it to… from here?	**Wie weit ist es von hier nach…?**	vee vight ist ehss fon heer nahkh
Can you tell me, where… is?	**Können Sie mir sagen, wo… ist?**	kurnern zee meer zargern voa … ist
Where can I find this address?	**Wie komme ich zu dieser Adresse?**	vee kommer ikh tsu deezer ahdrehsser
Where's this?	**Wo ist das?**	voa ist dahss

Miles into kilometres

1 mile = 1.609 kilometres (km.)

miles	10	20	30	40	50	60	70	80	90	100
km.	16	32	48	64	80	97	113	129	145	161

Kilometres into miles

1 kilometre (km.) = 0.62 miles

km.	10	20	30	40	50	60	70	80	90	100	110	120	130
miles	6	12	19	25	31	37	44	50	56	62	68	75	81

Can you show me on the map where I am?	Können Sie mir auf der Karte zeigen, wo ich bin?	kurnern zee meer owf derr **kahrter tsigh**gern voa ikh bin
Can you show me on the map where the university is?	Können Sie mir auf der Karte zeigen, wo die Universität ist?	kurnern zee meer owf derr **kahrter tsigh**gern voa dee unnivvehrzit**tait** ist
Can I park there?	Kann man dort parken?	kahn mahn dort **pahr**kern
Is that a one-way street?	Ist das eine Einbahnstraße?	ist dahss **ighner ighn**barnshtrarsser
Does the traffic go this way?	Ist dies die Fahrtrichtung?	ist deess dee **farrt**rikhtung

Sie sind auf der falschen Straße.	You're on the wrong road.
Fahren Sie geradeaus.	Go straight ahead.
Es ist dort unten...	It's down there on the...
links/rechts	left/right
Fahren Sie bis zur ersten (zweiten) Kreuzung.	Go to the first (second) crossroads.
Biegen Sie bei der Ampel links ab.	Turn left at the traffic lights.
Biegen Sie bei der nächsten Ecke rechts ab.	Turn right at the next corner.

CAR—INFORMATION

In the rest of this section we'll be more closely concerned with the car itself. We've divided it into two parts:

Part A contains general advice on motoring in Germany, Austria and Switzerland. It's essentially for reference and is therefore to be browsed over, preferably in advance.

Part B is concerned with the practical details of accidents and breakdown. It includes a list of car parts and a list of things that may go wrong with them. All you have to do is to show it to the garage mechanic and get him to point to the items required.

Part A
Customs—Documentation

You'll need the following documents when driving in Germany, Austria and Switzerland:

    passport
    international insurance certificate (green card)
    log book (car registration card)
    valid driving licence

The nationality plate or sticker must be on the car. Since some countries require a translation of your home driving licence, an international driving permit may save you trouble.

A red warning triangle—for display on the road in case of accident—is compulsory; seatbelts must be worn. Crash helmets are mandatory for both riders and passengers on motorcycles and scooters.

Here's my...	Hier ist...	heer ist
customs pass	**meine Zoll-bescheinigung**	**migh**ner **tsol**bershigh-niggung
driving licence	**mein Führerschein**	mighn **few**rerrshighn
green card	**meine grüne Ver-sicherungskarte**	**migh**ner **grew**ner fehr-zikherrungskahrter
passport	**mein Paß**	mighn pahss
log book (car registration card)	**mein Kraftfahrzeug-schein**	mighn **krahft**fahrtsoyg-shighn

Driving

The classification of roads in Germany is as follows:

E. 4	**Europastraße**—international road or motorway (turnpike)	
BAB	**Bundesautobahn** motorway (turnpike)	
B. 5	**Bundesstraße**—first-class main road	
L. 162	**Landesstraße**—second-class main road	
K. 27	**Kreisstraße**—district road	

The roads are good in Germany, Austria and Switzerland. There's an extensive network of motorways (turnpikes), which are all toll-free. At regular intervals along many motorways there are 24-hour telephone posts for emergencies, breakdown and accidents.

The same rules and regulations as in Germany generally apply on Austrian and Swiss roads. But on mountain roads there are some courtesies to be kept in mind: when two vehicles meet on very narrow roads the ascending vehicle has priority over the descending one. Try to keep a lookout ahead so that you can pull in to the side at some suitable spot before meeting the other vehicle. You must wherever possible give way to busses and other heavy vehicles.

As half of Switzerland and three-fourths of Austria are mountainous, don't forget to exercice particular caution on mountain roads where visibility may be impaired due to sharp bends and haze. In winter, make sure to check on driving conditions as some roads are temporarily closed, and wintry storms can make roads hazardous from October to May. Snow tires or chains are obligatory in some areas. In winter, if you dial 163 in Switzerland, a recorded message in German reports current road conditions for the region.

As in Germany, you'll find roads in Austria and Switzerland usually very well paved and marked for the motorist—though village roads may be narrow and require careful driving.

The police are normally quite lenient with tourists, but don't push your luck too far. For small offences you can be fined on the spot. Here are some phrases which may come in handy in case of confrontation with the *Polizei*. If you're in serious trouble, insist on an interpreter.

I'm sorry, officer, I didn't see the sign.	**Es tut mir leid, ich habe das Zeichen nicht gesehen.**	ehss toot meer light ikh **har**ber dahss **tsigh**khern nikht ger**zay**ern
The light was green.	**Die Ampel war grün.**	dee **ahm**perl varr grewn
I'm sorry, I don't speak German very well.	**Es tut mir leid, ich spreche nur wenig Deutsch.**	ehss toot meer light ikh **shpreh**kher noor **vay**nikh doych
I don't understand.	**Ich verstehe nicht.**	ikh vehr**shtay**er nikht
How much is the fine?	**Wie hoch ist die Buße?**	vee hoakh ist dee **boos**ser

Parking

Use your common sense when parking. Park your vehicle in the direction of moving traffic, not against it. Obey the parking regulations which will be indicated by signs or by lines painted on the kerb (curb).

When you park in the mountains in winter it's best to leave your car in gear but not to put the hand brake on. This will prevent the brake shoes from being frozen in in this position.

Excuse me. May I park here?	**Verzeihung, darf ich hier parken?**	fehrt**sigh**ung dahrf ikh heer **pahr**kern
How long can I park here?	**Wie lange kann ich hier parken?**	vee **lahng**er kahn ikh heer **pahr**kern
Do I have to leave my lights on?	**Muß ich das Parklicht brennen lassen?**	muss ikh dahss **pahrk**likht **breh**nern **lah**ssern
Excuse me. Do you have some change for the parking meter?	**Verzeihung, haben Sie zufällig Kleingeld für die Parkuhr?**	fehrt**sigh**ung **har**bern zee **tsoo**fehlikh **klighn**gehlt fewr dee **pahr**koor

Road signs

Listed below are some written signs which you'll certainly encounter when driving in Germany. Obviously, they should be studied in advance. You can't drive and read at the same time !

AUF 10 KM	Indicates that a sign applies for 10 kilometres
BLAUE ZONE	Blue zone (parking); special parking disc required
DURCHGANGSVERKEHR	Through traffic
EINBAHNSTRASSE	One-way street
EINORDNEN	Get in lane
ENDE DES PARKVERBOTS	End of no-parking zone
...ERLAUBT	...permitted
FROSTSCHÄDEN	Ice damage
FUSSGÄNGER	Pedestrians
GEFÄHRLICHES GEFÄLLE	Steep descent
GEFÄHRLICHE STEIGUNG	Steep climb
HALT, POLIZEI	Stop, police
HUPEN VERBOTEN	No honking
KEIN DURCHGANG FÜR FUSSGÄNGER	No pedestrians
KURZPARKZONE	Limited parking zone
LAWINENGEFAHR	Avalanche area
LINKS FAHREN	Keep left
LKW	Alternative route for heavy vehicles
NUR FÜR ANLIEGER	Access to residents only
PARKEN VERBOTEN	No parking
RECHTS FAHREN	Keep right
SCHLECHTE FAHRBAHN	Bad road surface
SCHULE	School
STEINSCHLAG	Falling rocks
STRASSENARBEITEN	Road works ahead (men working)
UMLEITUNG	Diversion (detour)
...VERBOTEN	No...
VORSICHT	Caution
WIRD EINGEFAHREN	Running-in (breaking-in) motor

FOR INTERNATIONAL ROAD SIGNS, see pages 160-161

Part B

Accidents

This section is confined to immediate aid. The legal problems of responsibility and settlement can be taken care of at a later stage. Your first concern will be for the injured.

Is anyone hurt?	**Ist jemand verletzt?**	ist **yay**mahnt fehr**leht**st
Don't move.	**Bewegen Sie sich nicht.**	ber**vay**gern zee zikh nikht
It's all right. Don't worry.	**Es geht gut. Keine Sorge.**	ehss gayt goot. **kigh**ner **zor**ger
Where's the nearest telephone?	**Wo ist das nächste Telephon?**	voa ist dahss **nehkh**ster **tay**lay**foan**
Can I use your telephone? There's been an accident.	**Kann ich Ihr Telephon benutzen? Es hat einen Unfall gegeben.**	kahn ikh eer **tay**lay**foan** ber**nut**sern? ehss haht **igh**nern **un**fahl ger**gay**bern
Call a doctor (an ambulance) immediately.	**Rufen Sie schnell einen Arzt (einen Krankenwagen).**	**roo**fern zee shnehl **igh**nern ahrst (**igh**nern **krahng**kern**var**gern)
There are people injured.	**Es hat Verletzte gegeben.**	ehss haht fehr**leht**ster ger**gay**bern
Help me get them out of the car.	**Helfen Sie mir, sie aus dem Wagen zu holen.**	**hehl**fern zee meer zee owss daym **var**gern tsu **hoa**lern

Police—Exchange of information

Please call the police.	**Rufen Sie bitte die Polizei.**	**roo**fern zee **bit**ter dee poa**lit**sigh
There's been an accident. It's about 2 km. from...	**Es ist ein Unfall passiert, ungefähr 2 Kilometer von...**	ehss ist ighn **un**fahl pah**sseert** **un**ger**fair** 2 kil**loam**may**terr** fon
I'm on the Frankfurt–Cologne motorway (expressway), 25 km. from Cologne.	**Ich bin auf der Autobahn Frankfurt–Köln, 25 Kilometer von Köln.**	ikh bin owf derr **ow**toabahn **frahngk**foort–kurln 25 kil**loam**may**terr** fon kurln
Here's my name and address.	**Hier ist mein Name und meine Adresse.**	heer ist mighn **nar**mer unt **migh**ner ah**dreh**sser

| Would you mind acting as a witness? | **Würden Sie bitte als Zeuge auftreten?** | vewrdern zee bitter ahlss tsoyger owftraytern |
| I'd like an interpreter. | **Ich hätte gern einen Dolmetscher.** | ikh hehter gehrn ighnern dolmehtsherr |

Remember to put out a red warning triangle if the car is out of action or impeding traffic.

Breakdown

...and that's what we'll do with this section: break it down into four phases.

1. *On the road*
   You ask where the nearest garage is.

2. *At the garage*
   You tell the mechanic what's wrong.

3. *Finding the trouble*
   He tells you what he thinks is wrong.

4. *Getting it repaired*
   You tell him to repair it, and once that's over settle the account (or argue about it).

Phase 1—On the road

Where's the nearest garage?	**Wo ist die nächste Reparaturwerkstatt?**	voa ist dee nehkhster raypahrahtoorvehrkshtaht
Excuse me. My car has broken down. May I use your phone?	**Entschuldigung, mein Wagen hat eine Panne. Darf ich Ihr Telephon benutzen?**	ehntshuldigung mighn vargern haht ighner pahner. dahrf ikh eer taylayfoan bernutsern
What's the telephone number of the nearest garage?	**Welche Telephonnummer hat die nächste Reparaturwerkstatt?**	vehlkher taylayfoannummerr haht dee nehkhster raypahrahtoorvehrkshtaht
I've had a breakdown at...	**Ich habe eine Panne in...**	ikh harber ighner pahner in

Can you send a mechanic?	**Können Sie einen Mechaniker schicken?**	kurnern zee ighnern mehkhanikkerr shikkern
Can you send a truck to tow my car?	**Können Sie einen Abschleppwagen schicken?**	kurnern zee ighnern ahpshlehpvargern shikkern
How long will you be?	**Wie lange dauert es?**	vee langer dowerrt ehss

Phase 2—At the garage

Can you help me?	**Können Sie mir helfen?**	kurnern zee meer hehlfern
I don't know what's wrong with it.	**Ich weiß nicht, was mit dem Wagen los ist.**	ikh vighss nikht vahss mit daym vargern loass ist
I think there's something wrong with the...	**Ich glaube, ... ist/sind nicht in Ordnung.**	ikh glowber ... ist/zint nikht in ortnung
battery	**die Batterie**	dee bahtehree
brakes	**die Bremsen**	dee brehmzern
bulbs	**die Glühbirnen**	dee glewbirnern
carburettor	**der Vergaser**	derr fehrgarzerr
clutch	**die Kupplung**	dee kuplung
cooling system	**die Kühlung**	dee kewlung
contact	**der Kontakt**	derr kontahkt
dipswitch (dimmer)	**der Abblendschalter**	derr ahpblehntschahlterr
dynamo	**die Lichtmaschine**	dee likhtmahsheener
electrical system	**die elektrische Anlage**	dee ehlehktrisher ahnlarger
engine	**der Motor**	derr moatoar
exhaust pipe	**das Auspuffrohr**	dahss owspufroar
fan	**der Ventilator**	derr vehntillartoar
filter	**der Filter**	derr filterr
fuel pump	**die Benzinpumpe**	dee behntseenpumper
fuel tank	**der Benzintank**	derr behntseentahnk
gear shift	**die Gangschaltung**	dee gahngshahltung
generator	**die Lichtmaschine**	dee likhtmahsheener
hand brake	**die Handbremse**	dee hahntbrehmzer
headlights	**die Scheinwerfer**	dee shighnvehrferr
heating	**die Heizung**	dee hightsung
horn	**die Hupe**	dee hooper
ignition system	**die Zündung**	dee tsewndung
indicator	**der Blinker**	derr blinkerr

lights	die Beleuchtung	dee berloykhtung
back-up lights	Rückfahrleuchten	rewkfarrloykhtern
brake lights	Bremsleuchten	brehmsloykhtern
rear lights	Schlußleuchten	shlusloykhtern
reversing lights	Rückfahrleuchten	rewkfarrloykhtern
tail lights	Schlußleuchten	shlusloykhtern
lines	die Leitungen	dee lightungern
lining and covering	der Bremsbelag und Bremsschutz	derr brehmsberlarg unt brehmsshuts
lubrication system	das Schmiersystem	dahss shmeersistaym
parking brake	die Handbremse	dee hahntbrehmzer
radiator	der Kühler	derr kewlerr
seat	der Sitz	derr zits
sliding roof	das Schiebedach	dahss sheeberdahkh
sparking plugs	die Zündkerzen	dee tsewntkehrtsern
speedometer	der Tachometer	derr tahkhommayterr
starter	der Anlasser	derr ahnlahsserr
steering	die Lenkung	dee lehngkung
suspension	die Federung	dee fayderrung
transmission	das Getriebe	dahss gertreeber
turn signal	der Blinker	derr blingkerr
wheels	die Räder	dee raiderr
wipers	die Scheibenwischer	dee shighbernvisherr

LEFT	RIGHT		FRONT	BACK
LINKS	RECHTS		VORNE	HINTEN
(links)	(rehkhts)		(forner)	(hintern)

It's...	Es...	ehss
bad	ist schadhaft	ist shardhaft
blowing	schließt nicht	shleest nikht
blown	ist durchgebrannt	ist doorkhgebrahnt
broken	ist gebrochen	ist gerbrokhern
burnt	ist verbrannt	ist fehrbrahnt
cracked	ist gesprungen	ist gershprungern
defective	ist defekt	ist dayfehkt
disconnected	ist losgelöst	ist losgerlurst
dry	ist trocken	ist trokkern
frozen	ist eingefroren	ist ighngerfroarern
jammed	ist blockiert	ist blokkeert
knocking	klopft	klopft
leaking	ist undicht	ist undikht
loose	ist lose	ist loazer

misfiring	**gibt Fehlzündungen**	gipt **faylt**sewndungern
noisy	**ist zu laut**	ist tsu lowt
not working	**funktioniert nicht**	funktsion**neert** nikht
overheating	**ist überhitzt**	ist ewber**hitst**
short-circuiting	**hat Kurzschluß**	hat **koorts**shluss
slack	**ist locker**	ist **lok**kerr
slipping	**rutscht**	rucht
stuck	**ist verklemmt**	ist fehr**klehmt**
vibrating	**vibriert**	vi**breert**
weak	**ist zu schwach**	ist tsu shvahkh
worn	**ist verschlissen**	ist fehr**shlissern**
The car won't start.	**Der Wagen springt nicht an.**	derr **var**gern shpringt nikht ahn
It's locked and the keys are inside.	**Er ist abgeschlossen und die Schlüssel sind drinnen.**	err ist ahp**gershlossern** unt dee **shlews**serl zint **drinnern**
The fan belt is too slack.	**Der Keilriemen ist zu schlaff.**	derr **kighl**reemern ist tsu shlahf
The radiator is leaking.	**Der Kühler ist undicht.**	derr **kew**lerr ist **un**dikht
I want maintenance and lubrication service.	**Ich möchte Wartungs- und Schmierdienst.**	ikh **murkh**ter **vahr**tungs-unt **shmeer**deenst
The idling needs adjusting.	**Der Leerlauf muß eingestellt werden.**	derr **layr**lowf muss **ighn**gershtehlt **vayr**dern
The clutch engages too quickly.	**Die Kupplung greift zu schnell.**	dee **kup**lung **grighft** tsu shnehl
The steering wheel's vibrating.	**Das Steuerrad vibriert.**	dahss **shtoyer**rrrad vi**breert**
The wipers are smearing.	**Die Scheibenwischer schmieren.**	dee **shighb**ernvisherr **shmeer**ern
The pneumatic suspension is weak.	**Die Luftdruckfederung ist zu weich.**	dee **luft**drukfayderrung ist tsu **vighkh**

Now that you've explained what's wrong, you'll want to know how long it'll take to repair it and make your arrangements accordingly.

How long will it take to repair?	**Wie lange dauert die Reparatur?**	vee **lahng**er **dow**errt dee raypahrah**toor**

How long will it take to find out what's wrong?	**Wie lange brauchen Sie, um den Fehler zu finden?**	vee lahnger browkhern zee um dayn faylerr tsu findern
Suppose I come back in half an hour?	**Kann ich in einer halben Stunde zurückkommen?**	kahn ikh in ighnerr hahlbern shtunder tsoorewkkommern
Can you give me a lift into town?	**Können Sie mich in die Stadt fahren?**	kurnern zee mikh in dee shtaht farrern
Is there a place to stay nearby?	**Kann man hier in der Nähe übernachten?**	kahn mahn heer in derr naier ewberrnahkhtern

Phase 3—Finding the trouble

It's up to the mechanic either to find the trouble or to repair it. All you have to do is hand him the book and point to the text in German below.

Bitte sehen Sie in dieser alphabetisch geordneten Liste nach, und weisen Sie auf das, was am Wagen nicht in Ordnung ist. Wenn Ihr Kunde wissen will, was damit los ist, zeigen Sie ihm den zutreffenden Ausdruck in der nächsten Liste (gebrochen, Kurzschluß usw.).*

Abblendschalter	dipswitch (dimmer switch)
automatisches Getriebe	automatic transmission
Batterie	battery
Batterieflüssigkeit	battery liquid
Batteriezellen	battery cells
Belag	lining
Benzinfilter	fuel filter
Benzinpumpe	fuel pump
Bremsbacken	brake shoes
Bremse	brake
Bremstrommel	brake drum
destilliertes Wasser	distilled water
Druckfedern	pressure springs
Einspritzpumpe	injection pump

* Please look at the following alphabetical list and point to the defective item. If your customer wants to know what's wrong with it, pick the applicable term from the next list (broken, short-circuited, etc.)

CAR—REPAIRS

Elektrische Anlage	electrical system
Federn	springs
Federung	suspension
Filter	filter
Gangschaltung	gear shift
Gelenk	joint
Getriebe	gearbox (transmission)
Getriebegehäuse	transmission case
Hauptlager	main bearings
Kabel	cable
Kardangelenk	universal joint
Kolben	piston
Kolbenringe	piston rings
Kondensator	condensor
Kontakt	contact
Kühler	radiator
Kühlung	cooling system
Kupplung	clutch
Kupplungspedal	clutch pedal
Kupplungsscheibe	clutch plate
Kurbelwelle	crankshaft
Kurbelwellengehäuse	crankcase
Lenkgehäuse	steering box
Lenksäule	steering column
Lichtmaschine	dynamo (generator)
Luftdruckfederung	pneumatic suspension
Luftfilter	air filter
Membrane	diaphragm
Motor	engine
Motorblock	block
Nockenwelle	camshaft
Ölfilter	oil filter
Ölpumpe	oil pump
Pumpe	pump
Räder	wheels
Schmierfett	grease
Schwimmer	float
Spurstangenenden	track rod ends
Stabilisator	stabilizer
Starter	starter motor
Steuerung	steering
Stoßdämpfer	shock-absorber
Stößel	tappets
Stoßstange	fender (bumper)
Thermostat	thermostat
Ventil	valve
Ventilator	fan

Ventilfeder	valve spring
Vergaser	carburettor
Verteiler	distributor
Verteilerfinger	distributor leads
Wasserpumpe	water pump
Welle	shaft
Zähne	teeth
Zahnstangengetriebe	rack and pinion
Zündkerzen	sparking plugs
Zündkerzenkabel	sparking-plug leads
Zündspule	ignition coil
Zylinder	cylinder
Zylinderkopf	cylinder head
Zylinderkopfdichtung	cylinder-head gasket

Die Ausdrücke in der folgenden Liste helfen Ihnen, zu erklären, was nicht in Ordnung ist und wie man den Schaden beheben kann.*

abgenutzt	worn
anziehen	to tighten
aufladen	to charge
ausbauen	to strip down
auswechseln	to change
auswuchten	to balance
blockiert	jammed
defekt	defective
durchgebrannt	blown
einschleifen	to grind in
entlüften	to bleed
ersetzen	to replace
Fehlzündung haben	misfiring
gefroren	frozen
gesprungen	cracked
(zu) hoch	(too) high
kaputt	broken
klopft	knocking
(zu) kurz	(too) short
Kurzschluß haben	short-circuited
lockern	to loosen
lose	loose
losgelöst	disconnected
nachstellen	to adjust

* The following list contains words which describe what's wrong as well as what may need to be done.

neubelegen	to reline
(zu) niedrig	(too) low
reinigen	to clean
rutscht	slipping
(zu) schlaff	(too) slack
schließt nicht	blowing
(zu) schnell	(too) quick
(zu) schwach	(too) weak
Spiel haben	play
trocken	dry
überhitzt	overheating
undicht	leaking
verbogen	warped
verbrannt	burnt
verklemmt	stuck
verrostet	corroded
verschmutzt	dirty
vibriert	vibrating

Phase 4—Getting it repaired

| Have you found the trouble? | **Haben Sie den Fehler gefunden?** | harbern zee dayn faylerr gerfundern |

Now that you know what's wrong, or at least have some idea, you'll want to find out...

Is that serious?	**Ist das schlimm?**	ist dahss shlim
Can you repair it?	**Können Sie es reparieren?**	kurnern zee ehss raypahreerern
Can you do it now?	**Können Sie es sofort reparieren?**	kurnern zee ehss zoafort raypahreerern
What's it going to cost?	**Was wird es kosten?**	vahss veert ehss kostern
Do you have the necessary spare parts?	**Haben Sie die nötigen Ersatzteile?**	harbern zee dee nurtiggern ehrzahtstighler

What if he says "no"?

| Why can't you do it? | **Warum können Sie es nicht reparieren?** | vahrum kurnern zee ehss nikht raypahreerern |
| Is it essential to have that part? | **Geht es nicht ohne dieses Ersatzteil?** | gayt ehss nikht oaner deezerss ehrzahtstighl |

How long is it going to take to get the spare parts?	Wie lange brauchen Sie für die Beschaffung der Ersatzteile?	vee **lahng**er **brow**khern zee fewr dee ber**shahf**fung derr ehr**zahts**tighler
Where's the nearest garage that can repair it?	Wo ist die nächste Werkstatt, die das reparieren kann?	voa ist dee **nehkh**ster **vehrk**shtaht dee dahss raypah**ree**rern kahn
Can you fix it so that I can get as far as...?	Können Sie es so reparieren, dass ich noch bis...komme?	**kur**nern zee ehss zoa raypah**ree**rern dahss ikh nokh biss ... **kom**mer

If you're really stuck, ask if you can leave the car at the garage. Contact an automobile association or hire another car.

Settling the bill

| Is everything fixed? | Ist der Schaden behoben? | ist derr **shar**dern ber**hoa**bern |
| How much do I owe you? | Was schulde ich Ihnen? | vahss **shul**der ikh **ee**nern |

The garage then presents you with the bill. If you're satisfied...

Will you take a traveller's cheque?	Nehmen Sie Reisechecks?	**nay**mern zee **righ**zershehks
Thanks very much for your help.	Vielen Dank für Ihre Hilfe.	**fee**lern dahnk fewr **ee**rer **hil**fer
This is for you.	Das ist für Sie.	dahss ist fewr zee

But you may feel that the workmanship is sloppy or that you're paying for work not done. Get the bill itemized. If necessary, get it translated before you pay.

| I'd like to check the bill first. Will you itemize the work done? | Ich möchte die Rechnung erst prüfen. Können Sie die Arbeit spezifizieren? | ikh **murkh**ter dee **rehkh**nung ehrst **prew**fern. **kur**nern zee dee **ahr**bight shpehtsiffit**seer**ern |

If the garage still won't back down and you're sure you're right, get the help of a third party.

Some international road signs

No vehicles

No entry

No overtaking (passing)

Oncoming traffic has priority

Maximum speed limit

No parking

Caution

Intersection

Dangerous bend (curve)

Road narrows

Intersection with secondary road

Two-way traffic

Dangerous hill

Uneven road

Falling rocks

Give way (yield)

Main road,
thoroughfare

End of restriction

One-way traffic

Traffic goes
this way

Roundabout
(rotary)

Bicycles only

Pedestrians
only

Minimum speed
limit

Keep right
(left if symbol
reversed)

Parking

Hospital

Motorway
(expressway)

Motor vehicles
only

Filling station

No through road

Doctor

Frankly, how much use is a phrase book going to be to you in case of serious injury or illness? The only phrase you need in such an emergency is...

Get a doctor quickly!	**Rufen Sie schnell einen Arzt!**	roofern zee shnehl ighnern ahrtst

But there are minor aches and pains, ailments and irritations that can upset the best-planned trip. Here we can help you and, perhaps, the doctor.

Some doctors will speak English well; others will know enough for your needs. But suppose there's something the doctor can't explain because of language difficulties? We've thought of that. As you'll see, this section has been arranged to enable you and the doctor to communicate. From pages 165 to 171, you find your part of the dialogue on the upper half of each page—the doctor's is on the lower half.

The whole section has been divided into three parts: illness, wounds, nervous tension. Page 171 is concerned with prescriptions and fees.

General

I need a doctor quickly.	**Ich brauche schnell einen Arzt.**	ikh browkher shnehl ighnern ahrtst
Can you get me a doctor?	**Können Sie einen Arzt für mich finden?**	kurnern zee ighnern ahrtst fewr mikh findern
Is there a doctor here?	**Gibt es hier einen Arzt?**	gipt ehss heer ighnern ahrtst
Please telephone for a doctor immediately.	**Bitte rufen Sie sofort einen Arzt an.**	bitter roofern zee zoafort ighnern ahrtst ahn
Where's there a doctor who speaks English?	**Wo gibt es einen Arzt, der Englisch spricht?**	voa gipt ehss ighnern ahrtst derr ehnglish shprikht

DOCTOR

Where's the surgery (doctor's office)?	**Wo ist die Arztpraxis?**	voa ist dee **ahrtst**prahksiss
What are the surgery (office) hours?	**Wann sind die Sprechstunden?**	vahn zint dee **shprekh**shtundern
Could the doctor come to see me here?	**Könnte der Arzt mich hier behandeln?**	kurnter derr ahrtst mikh heer ber**hahn**derln
What time can the doctor come?	**Wann kann der Arzt kommen?**	vahn kahn derr ahrtst **kommern**

Symptoms

Use this section to tell the doctor what's wrong. Basically, what he'll require to know is:

> **What?** (ache, pain, bruise, etc.)
> **Where?** (arm, stomach, etc.)
> **How long?** (have you had the trouble)

Before you visit the doctor, find out the answers to these questions by glancing through the pages that follow. In this way, you'll save time.

Parts of the body

ankle	**der Knöchel**	derr **knurk**herl
appendix	**der Blinddarm**	derr **blint**dahrm
arm	**der Arm**	derr ahrm
artery	**die Arterie**	dee ahr**tay**rier
back	**der Rücken**	derr **rew**kern
bladder	**die Blase**	dee **blar**zer
blood	**das Blut**	dahss bloot
bone	**der Knochen**	derr **knok**hern
bowels	**der Darm**	derr dahrm
breast	**die Brust**	dee brust
cheek	**die Backe**	dee **bah**ker
chest	**der Brustkorb**	derr **brust**korp
chin	**das Kinn**	dahss kin
collar-bone	**das Schlüsselbein**	dahss **shlewss**erlbighn
ear	**das Ohr**	dahss oar
elbow	**der Ellbogen**	derr **ehl**boagern
eye	**das Auge**	dahss **ow**ger
face	**das Gesicht**	dahss ger**zikht**
finger	**der Finger**	derr **finger**r

DOCTOR

foot	der Fuß	derr fooss
forehead	die Stirn	dee shteern
gland	die Drüse	dee drewzer
hair	das Haar	dahss harr
hand	die Hand	dee hahnt
head	der Kopf	derr kopf
heart	das Herz	dahss hehrts
heel	die Ferse	dee fehrzer
hip	die Hüfte	dee hewfter
intestines	die Eingeweide	dee ighngervighder
jaw	der Kiefer	derr keeferr
joint	das Gelenk	dahss gerlehngk
kidney	die Niere	dee neerer
knee	das Knie	dahss knee
knee cap	die Kniescheibe	dee kneeshighber
leg	das Bein	dahss bighn
lip	die Lippe	dee lipper
liver	die Leber	dee layberr
lung	die Lunge	dee lunger
mouth	der Mund	derr munt
muscle	der Muskel	derr muskerl
neck	der Hals	derr hahls
nerve	der Nerv	derr nehrf
nervous system	das Nervensystem	dahss nehrfernzewstaym
nose	die Nase	dee narzer
rib	die Rippe	dee ripper
shoulder	die Schulter	dee shulterr
skin	die Haut	dee howt
spine	die Wirbelsäule	dee veerberlzoyler
stomach	der Magen	derr margern
tendon	die Sehne	dee zayner
thigh	der Schenkel	derr shehngkerl
throat	der Hals	derr hahls
thumb	der Daumen	derr dowmern
toe	die Zehe	dee tsayer
tongue	die Zunge	dee tsunger
tonsils	die Mandeln	dee mahnderln
urine	der Urin	derr ooreen
vein	die Vene	dee vayner
wrist	das Handgelenk	dahss hahntgerlehnk

the left.../on the left side	the right.../on the right side
der/die/das linke.../links	**der/die/das rechte.../rechts**
(der/dee/dahss **ling**ker/links)	(derr/dee/dahss **rehkh**ter/rehkhts)

PATIENT
Part 1—Illness

I'm not feeling well.	Ich fühle mich nicht wohl.	ikh **few**ler mikh nikht voal
I'm ill.	Ich bin krank.	ikh bin krahngk
I've got a pain here.	Ich habe hier Schmerzen.	ikh **hah**ber heer **shmehrts**ern
His / Her...hurts.	Sein/Ihr...tut weh.	zighn/eer ... toot vay
I've got (a)...	Ich habe...	ikh **hah**ber
backache	Rückenschmerzen	**rew**kernshmehrtsern
fever	Fieber	**fee**berr
headache	Kopfschmerzen	**kopfsh**mehrtsern
sore throat	Halsschmerzen	**hahlssh**mehrtsern
travel sickness	Reisekrankheit	**righ**zerkrahngk-hight
I'm constipated.	Ich habe Verstopfung.	ikh **hah**ber fehr**shtop**fung
I've been vomiting.	Ich habe mich übergeben.	ikh **hah**ber mikh **ewberrgay**bern

---

DOCTOR
1—Krankheit

Was fehlt Ihnen?	What's the trouble?
Wo haben Sie Schmerzen?	Where does it hurt?
Wie lange haben Sie diese Schmerzen schon?	How long have you had this pain?
Wie lange fühlen Sie sich schon so?	How long have you been feeling like this?
Streifen Sie den Ärmel hoch.	Roll up your sleeve.
Bitte machen Sie den Oberkörper frei.	Please undress down to the waist.
Ziehen Sie bitte Hose und Unterhose aus.	Please remove your trousers and underpants.

PATIENT

I feel faint / I feel dizzy.	Ich fühle mich schwach/Mir ist schwindlig.	ikh **fewler** mikh shvahkh/meer ist **shvindlikh**
I'm nauseous.	**Mir ist übel.**	meer ist **ewberl**
I feel shivery.	**Mich fröstelt.**	mikh **frursterlt**
I've/He's got/She's got (a/an)...	**Ich habe/Er hat/Sie hat...**	ikh **harber**/ehr haht/ zee haht
abscess	einen Abszeß	**ighnern** ahp**stsehss**
asthma	Asthma	**ahst**mah
boil	einen Furunkel	**ighnern** foo**rung**kerl
cold	eine Erkältung	**ighner** ehr**kehl**tung
constipation	Verstopfung	fehr**shtop**fung
cramps	Krämpfe	**krehm**pfer
diarrhoea	Durchfall	**doorkh**fahl
fever	Fieber	**fee**berr
haemorrhoids	Hämorrhoiden	hehmoaroa**ee**dern
hay fever	Heufieber	**hoy**feeberr
hernia	einen Bruch	**ighnern** brukh

DOCTOR

Legen Sie sich bitte hierhin.	Please lie down over here.
Machen Sie den Mund auf.	Open your mouth.
Tief atmen, bitte.	Breathe deeply.
Husten Sie bitte.	Cough, please.
Ich werde Ihre Temperatur messen.	I'll take your temperature.
Ich werde Ihren Blutdruck messen.	I'm going to take your blood pressure.
Haben Sie das zum ersten Mal?	Is it the first time you've had this?
Ich gebe Ihnen eine Spritze.	I'll give you an injection.
Ich möchte eine Urinprobe (Stuhlprobe) von Ihnen.	I want a specimen of your urine (stools).

PATIENT

indigestion	eine Magen-verstimmung	ighner margern-fehrshtimmung
inflammation of...	eine ...entzündung	ighner ...ehnttsewndung
influenza	Grippe	gripper
morning sickness	morgendliches Erbrechen	morgerntlikherss ehrbrehkhern
rheumatism	Rheuma	roymah
stiff neck	einen steifen Nacken	ighnern shtighfern nahkern
sunburn	Sonnenbrand	zonnernbrahnt
sunstroke	einen Sonnenstich	ighnern zonnernshtikh
tonsillitis	Mandelentzündung	mahnderlehnttsewndung
ulcer	ein Geschwür	ighn gershvewr
whooping cough	Keuchhusten	koykhhoostern
It's nothing serious, I hope?	Es ist hoffentlich nichts Ernstes?	ehss ist hofferntlikh nikhts ehrnsterss
I'd like you to prescribe some medicine for me.	Ich möchte, daß Sie mir ein Medikament verschreiben.	ikh murkhter dahss zee meer ighn mehdikkahmehnt fehrshrighbern

---

DOCTOR

Sie brauchen sich keine Sorgen zu machen.	It's nothing to worry about.
Sie müssen...Tage im Bett bleiben.	You must stay in bed for... days.
Sie haben...	You've got (a/an)....
eine Erkältung/Grippe	cold/influenza
eine Lungenentzündung	pneumonia
Arthritis	arthritis
Blinddarmentzündung	appendicitis
Sie rauchen zuviel.	You're smoking too much.
Sie trinken zuviel.	You're drinking too much.
Sie müssen zu einer General-untersuchung ins Krankenhaus.	I want you to go to hospital for a general check-up.
Ich werde Ihnen ein Antibiotikum verschreiben.	I'll prescribe an antibiotic.

PATIENT

I'm a diabetic.	**Ich bin Diabetiker.**	ikh bin diah**bay**tikkerr
I've a cardiac condition.	**Ich habe ein Herzleiden.**	ikh **har**ber ighn **hehrts**lighdern
I had a heart attack in...	**Ich hatte einen Herzanfall im...**	ikh **hah**ter **igh**nern **hehrts**ahnfahl im
I'm allergic to...	**Ich bin gegen ... allergisch.**	ikh bin **gay**gern ... ah**lehr**gish
This is my usual medicine.	**Gewöhnlich nehme ich dieses Medikament.**	ger**vurn**likh **nay**mer ikh **dee**zerss maydikah**mehnt**
I need this medicine.	**Ich brauche dieses Medikament.**	ikh **brow**kher **dee**zerss maydikah**mehnt**
I'm expecting a baby.	**Ich erwarte ein Baby.**	ikh ehr**vahr**ter ighn **bay**bee
Can I travel?	**Kann ich reisen?**	kahn ikh **righ**zern

DOCTOR

Welche Dosis Insulin nehmen Sie?	What dose of insulin are you taking?
Einspritzung oder Tabletten?	Injection or oral?
Wie sind Sie behandelt worden?	What treatment have you been having?
Welches Medikament haben Sie genommen?	What medicine have you been taking?
Sie haben einen (leichten) Herzanfall gehabt.	You've had a (slight) heart attack.
...führen wir in Deutschland nicht. Dies ist ein ähnliches Mittel.	We don't use...in Germany. This is very similar.
Wann erwarten Sie das Baby?	When is the baby due?
Sie können nicht reisen bis...	You can't travel until...

PATIENT

Part 2—Wounds

I've got a/an... Could you have a look at it?	Ich habe... Bitte sehen Sie es mal an.	ikh harber ... bitter zayern zee ehss marl ahn
blister	eine Blase	ighner blarzer
boil	einen Furunkel	ighnern foorungkerl
bruise	eine Quetschung	ighner kvehtshung
burn	eine Brandwunde	ighner brahntvunder
cut	eine Schnittwunde	ighner shnitvunder
graze	eine Abschürfung	ighner ahpshewrfung
insect bite	einen Insektenstich	ighnern inzehkternshtikh
lump	eine Beule	ighher boyler
rash	einen Ausschlag	ighnern owsshlarg
sting	einen Stich	ighnern shtikh
swelling	eine Schwellung	ighner shvehlung
wound	eine Wunde	ighner vunder
I can't move... It hurts.	Ich kann... nicht bewegen. Es schmerzt.	ikh kahn ... nikht bervaygern. ehss shmehrtst

---

DOCTOR

2—Wunden

Es ist (nicht) infiziert.	It is (not) infected.
Sie haben einen Bandscheibenvorfall.	You've got a slipped disc.
Sie müssen geröntgt werden.	You'll need an X-ray.
Es ist...	It's...
gebrochen/verstaucht verrenkt/gerissen	broken/sprained dislocated/torn
Sie haben eine Muskelzerrung.	You've pulled a muscle.
Ich gebe Ihnen ein Anti- septikum. Es ist nichts Ernstes.	I'll give you an antiseptic. It's not serious.
In...Tagen möchte ich Sie wieder sehen.	I want you to come and see me in ... days' time.

PATIENT

Part 3—Nervous tension

I'm in a nervous state.	**Ich bin übernervös.**	ikh bin ewberrnehrvurss
I'm feeling depressed.	**Ich habe Depressionen.**	ikh harber dayprehssioanern
I want some sleeping pills.	**Ich brauche Schlaftabletten.**	ikh browkher shlarftahblehtern
I can't eat/I can't sleep.	**Ich kann nicht essen/Ich kann nicht schlafen.**	ikh kahn nikht ehssern/ikh kahn nikht shlarfern
I'm having nightmares.	**Ich habe Alpträume.**	ikh harber ahlptroymer
Can you prescribe a...?	**Können Sie mir ein ...verschreiben ?**	kurnern zee meer ighn... fehrshrighbern
sedative	**Beruhigungsmittel**	berrooiggungsmitterl
anti-depressant	**Mittel gegen Depressionen**	mitterl gaygern dayprehssioanern

DOCTOR

3—Unruhe/Nervosität

Sie leiden unter nervöser Spannung.	You're suffering from nervous tension.
Sie brauchen Ruhe.	You need a rest.
Welche Tabletten haben Sie genommen ?	What pills have you been taking ?
Wie viele pro Tag ?	How many a day ?
Wie lange fühlen Sie sich schon so ?	How long have you been feeling like this ?
Ich verschreibe Ihnen Tabletten.	I'll prescribe some pills.
Ich gebe Ihnen ein Beruhigungsmittel.	I'll give you a sedative.

DOCTOR

PATIENT

Prescriptions and dosage

What kind of medicine is this?	**Was für ein Medikament ist das?**	vahss fewr ighn maydikah**mehnt** ist dahss
How many times a day should I take it?	**Wie oft am Tag muß ich es nehmen?**	vee oft ahm targ muss ikh ehss **nay**mern
Must I swallow them whole?	**Muß ich sie ganz schlucken?**	muss ikh zee gahnts **shluk**kern

Fee

How much do I owe you?	**Wieviel bin ich Ihnen schuldig?**	vee**feel** bin ikh **ee**nern **shul**dikh
Do I pay you now or will you send me your bill?	**Soll ich gleich bezahlen oder schicken Sie mir die Rechnung?**	zol ikh glighkh bert**sar**lern oader **shik**kern zee meer dee **rehkh**nung
Thanks for your help, Doctor.	**Vielen Dank für Ihre Hilfe, Herr Doktor.**	**fee**lern dahnk fewr **ee**rer **hil**fer hehr **dok**toar

---

DOCTOR

Rezept und Dosis

Nehmen Sie von dieser Medizin ... Teelöffel alle ... Stunden.	Take ... teaspoons of this medicine every ... hours.
Nehmen Sie ... Tabletten mit einem Glas Wasser ...	Take ... pills with a glass of water ...
... mal täglich	... times a day
vor jeder Mahlzeit	before each meal
nach jeder Mahlzeit	after each meal
morgens	in the mornings
abends	at night

Honorar

Das macht ... Mark, bitte.	That's ... marks, please.
Bitte zahlen Sie gleich jetzt.	Please pay me now.
Ich schicke Ihnen die Rechnung.	I'll send you a bill.

FOR NUMBERS, see page 175

PATIENT

DOCTOR

Dentist

Can you recommend a good dentist?	Können Sie einen guten Zahnarzt empfehlen?	kurnern zee ighnern gootern tsarnahrtst ehmpfaylern
Can I make an (urgent) appointment to see Dr....?	Kann ich einen (dringenden) Termin bei Herrn Dr.... ausmachen?	kahn ikh ighnern (dringerndern) tehrmeen bigh hehrn doktoar ... owsmahkhern
I've a toothache.	Ich habe Zahnschmerzen.	ikh harber tsarnshmehrtsern
I've an abscess.	Ich habe einen Abszeß.	ikh harber ighnern ahpstsehss
This tooth hurts.	Dieser Zahn schmerzt.	deezerr tsarn shmehrtst
at the top	oben	oabern
at the bottom	unten	untern
in the front	vorne	forner
at the back	hinten	hintern
Can you fix it temporarily?	Können Sie ihn provisorisch behandeln?	kurnern zee een provvizoarish berhahnderln
I don't want it extracted.	Ich möchte ihn nicht ziehen lassen.	ikh murkhter een nikht tseeeern lahssern
I've lost a filling.	Ich habe eine Füllung verloren.	ikh harber ighner fewlung fehrloarern
The gum is very sore.	Das Zahnfleisch ist wund.	dahss tsarnflighsh ist vunt
The gum is bleeding.	Das Zahnfleisch blutet.	dahss tsarnflighsh blootert

Dentures

I've broken this denture.	Mein Gebiß ist zerbrochen.	mighn gerbiss ist tsehrbrokhern
Can you repair this denture?	Können Sie das Gebiß reparieren?	kurnern zee dahss gerbiss raypahreerern
When will it be ready?	Wann ist es fertig?	vahn ist ehss fehrtikh

Optician

I've broken my glasses.	**Meine Brille ist zerbrochen.**	mighner **brill**er ist tsehrbrokhern
Can you repair them for me?	**Können Sie sie reparieren?**	kurnern zee zee raypahreerern
When will they be ready?	**Wann ist sie fertig?**	vahn ist zee **fehr**tikh
Can you change the lenses?	**Können Sie die Gläser auswechseln?**	kurnern zee dee **glaiz**err **ows**vehkserln
I want tinted lenses.	**Ich möchte getönte Gläser.**	ikh **murkh**ter ger**turn**ter **glaiz**err
I want some contact lenses.	**Ich möchte Kontaktlinsen.**	ikh **murkh**ter kon**tahkt**linzern
I'd like to buy a pair of binoculars.	**Ich hätte gern einen Feldstecher.**	ikh **hehter** gehrn **ighn**ern **fehlt**shtehkherr
I'd like to buy a pair of sun-glasses.	**Ich hätte gern eine Sonnenbrille.**	ikh **hehter** gehrn **ighn**er **zonn**ernbriller
How much do I owe you?	**Wieviel schulde ich Ihnen?**	vee**feel** shulder ikh **een**ern
Do I pay you now or will you send me your bill?	**Soll ich jetzt bezahlen oder schicken Sie mir die Rechnung?**	zol ikh yehtst bert**sar**lern oader **shikk**ern zee meer dee **rehkh**nung

FOR NUMBERS, see page 175

Reference section

Where do you come from?

Africa	**Afrika**	ahfrikkah
Asia	**Asien**	arziern
Australia	**Australien**	owstrarliern
Austria	**Österreich**	ursterrrighkh
Belgium	**Belgien**	behlgiern
Canada	**Kanada**	kahnahdah
China	**China**	kheenah
Czechoslovakia	**Tschechoslowakei**	chehkhosloavahkigh
Denmark	**Dänemark**	dainermahrk
England	**England**	ehnglahnt
Europe	**Europa**	oyroapah
France	**Frankreich**	frahngkrighkh
Federal Republic of Germany (West Germany)	**Bundesrepublik Deutschland**	bundesrehpublik doychlahnt
German Democratic Republic (East Germany)	**Deutsche Demokratische Republik**	doycher dehmokrartisher rehpublik
Germany	**Deutschland**	doychlahnt
Great Britain	**Großbritannien**	groasbrittahniern
Holland	**Holland**	hollahnt
Hungary	**Ungarn**	ungahrn
India	**Indien**	indiern
Ireland	**Irland**	eerlahnt
Italy	**Italien**	itarliern
Japan	**Japan**	yarparn
Liechtenstein	**Liechtenstein**	likhternshtighn
Luxemburg	**Luxemburg**	luksermboorg
New Zealand	**Neuseeland**	noyzaylahnt
North America	**Nordamerika**	nortahmayrikkah
Poland	**Polen**	poalern
Scandinavia	**Skandinavien**	skahndinnarviern
Scotland	**Schottland**	shotlahnt
South Africa	**Südafrika**	zewdahfrikkah
South America	**Südamerika**	zewdahmayrikkah
Soviet Union	**Sowjetunion**	zovyehtunnioan
Spain	**Spanien**	shparniern
Switzerland	**Schweiz**	shvights
United States	**Vereinigte Staaten**	fehrighnigter shtartern
Wales	**Wales**	"Wales"
Yugoslavia	**Jugoslawien**	yuggoslarviern

Numbers

0	null	nul
1	eins	ighns
2	zwei	tsvigh
3	drei	drigh
4	vier	feer
5	fünf	fewnf
6	sechs	zehks
7	sieben	zeebern
8	acht	ahkht
9	neun	noyn
10	zehn	tsayn
11	elf	ehlf
12	zwölf	tsvurlf
13	dreizehn	drightsayn
14	vierzehn	feertsayn
15	fünfzehn	fewnftsayn
16	sechzehn	zehkhtsayn
17	siebzehn	zeeptsayn
18	achtzehn	ahkhtsayn
19	neunzehn	noyntsayn
20	zwanzig	tsvahntsikh
21	einundzwanzig	ighnunttsvahntsikh
22	zweiundzwanzig	tsvighunttsvahntsikh
23	dreiundzwanzig	drighunttsvahntsikh
24	vierundzwanzig	feerunttsvahntsikh
25	fünfundzwanzig	fewnfunttsvahntsikh
26	sechsundzwanzig	zehksunttsvahntsikh
27	siebenundzwanzig	zeebernunttsvahntsikh
28	achtundzwanzig	ahkhtunttsvahntsikh
29	neunundzwanzig	noynunttsvahntsikh
30	dreißig	drighssikh
31	einunddreißig	ighnuntdrighssikh
32	zweiunddreißig	tsvighuntdrighssikh
33	dreiunddreißig	drighuntdrighssikh
40	vierzig	feertsikh
41	einundvierzig	ighnuntfeertsikh
42	zweiundvierzig	tsvighuntfeertsikh
43	dreiundvierzig	drighuntfeertsikh
50	fünfzig	fewnftsikh
51	einundfünfzig	ighnuntfewnftsikh
52	zweiundfünfzig	tsvighuntfewnftsikh
53	dreiundfünfzig	drighuntfewnftsikh
60	sechzig	zehkhtsikh
61	einundsechzig	ighnuntzehkhtsikh

62	**zweiundsechzig**	tsvighuntzehkhtsikh
63	**dreiundsechzig**	drighuntzehkhtsikh
70	**siebzig**	zeeptsikh
71	**einundsiebzig**	ighnuntzeeptsikh
72	**zweiundsiebzig**	tsvighuntzeeptsikh
73	**dreiundsiebzig**	drighuntzeeptsikh
80	**achtzig**	ahkhtsikh
81	**einundachtzig**	ighnuntahkhtsikh
82	**zweiundachtzig**	tsvighuntahkhtsikh
83	**dreiundachtzig**	drighuntahkhtsikh
90	**neunzig**	noyntsikh
91	**einundneunzig**	ighnuntnoyntsikh
92	**zweiundneunzig**	tsvighuntnoyntsikh
93	**dreiundneunzig**	drighuntnoyntsikh
100	**(ein)hundert**	(ighn)hunderrt
101	**hunderteins**	hunderrtighnss
102	**hundertzwei**	hunderrttsvigh
110	**hundertzehn**	hunderrttsayn
120	**hundertzwanzig**	hunderrttsvahntsikh
130	**hundertdreißig**	hunderrtdrighssikh
140	**hundertvierzig**	hunderrtfeertsikh
150	**hundertfünfzig**	hunderrtfewnftsikh
160	**hundertsechzig**	hunderrtzehkhtsikh
170	**hundertsiebzig**	hunderrtzeeptsikh
180	**hundertachtzig**	hunderrtahkhtsikh
190	**hundertneunzig**	hunderrtnoyntsikh
200	**zweihundert**	tsvighhunderrt
300	**dreihundert**	drighhunderrt
400	**vierhundert**	feerhunderrt
500	**fünfhundert**	fewnfhunderrt
600	**sechshundert**	zehkshunderrt
700	**siebenhundert**	zeebernhunderrt
800	**achthundert**	ahkhthunderrt
900	**neunhundert**	noynhunderrt
1000	**(ein)tausend**	(ighn) towzernt
1100	**tausendeinhundert**	towzerntighnhunderrt
1200	**tausendzweihundert**	towzernttsvighhunderrt
2000	**zweitausend**	tsvightowzernt
5000	**fünftausend**	fewnftowzernt
10,000	**zehntausend**	tsayntowzernt
50,000	**fünfzigtausend**	fewnftsikhtowzernt
100,000	**hunderttausend**	hunderrttowzernt
1,000,000	**eine Million**	ighner millioan
1,000,000,000	**eine Milliarde**	ighner milliahrder

first	**erste**	ehrster
second	**zweite**	tsvighter
third	**dritte**	dritter
fourth	**vierte**	feerter
fifth	**fünfte**	fewnfter
sixth	**sechste**	zehkster
seventh	**siebte**	zeebter
eighth	**achte**	ahkhter
ninth	**neunte**	noynter
tenth	**zehnte**	tsaynter
once	**einmal**	ighnmarl
twice	**zweimal**	tsvighmarl
three times	**dreimal**	drighmarl
half a...	**ein halber...**	ighn hahlberr
half of...	**die Hälfte von...**	dee hehlfter fon
half (adj.)	**halb**	hahlp
a quarter	**ein Viertel**	ighn feerterl
one third	**ein Drittel**	ighn dritterl
a pair of...	**ein Paar...**	ighn parr
a dozen	**ein Dutzend**	ighn dutsernd

1982 **neunzehnhundertzweiundachtzig**
(noyntsaynhunderrt**tsvigh**untahkhtsikh)

1983 **neunzehnhundertdreiundachtzig**
(noyntsaynhunderrt**drigh**untahkhtsikh)

1984 **neunzehnhundertvierundachtzig**
(noyntsaynhunderrt**feer**untahkhtsikh)

1985 **neunzehnhundertfünfundachtzig**
(noyntsaynhunderrt**fewnf**untahkhtsikh)

Time

viertel nach zwölf
(**feer**terl narkh tsvurlf)

zwanzig nach eins
(**tsvahn**tsikh narkh ighns)

fünf vor halb drei
(fewnf foar hahlp drigh)

halb vier
(hahlp feer)

fünf nach halb fünf
(fewnf narkh hahlp fewnf)

zwanzig vor sechs
(**tsvahn**tsikh foar zehks)

viertel vor sieben
(**feer**terl foar **zee**bern)

zehn vor acht
(tsayn foar ahkht)

fünf vor neun
(fewnf foar noyn)

zehn Uhr
(tsayn oor)

fünf nach elf
(fewnf narkh ehlf)

zehn nach zwölf
(tsayn narkh tsvurlf)

In ordinary conversation, time is expressed as above. However, official time uses a 24-hour clock which means that, after noon, hours are counted from 13 to 24. For instance, 13.15 would be 1.15 p.m. for us and 20.30 is 8.30 p.m. At midnight time returns to 0 so that 12.17 a.m. is written 0.17.

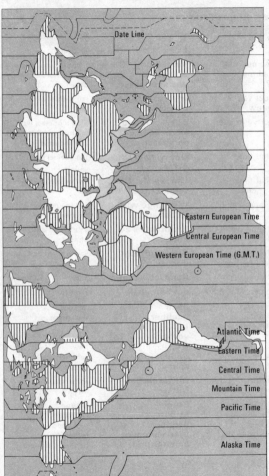

a.m. a.m. a.m. a.m. a.m. a.m. a.m. a.m. a.m. a.m. a.m. noon p.m. p.m. p.m. p.m. p.m. p.m. p.m. p.m. p.m. p.m. p.m. night

Date Line

Eastern European Time

Central European Time

Western European Time (G.M.T.)

Atlantic Time

Eastern Time

Central Time

Mountain Time

Pacific Time

Alaska Time

Countries which have adopted a time differing from that in the corresponding time zone. Note that also in the USSR, official time is one hour ahead of the time in each corresponding time zone. In summer, numerous countries advance time one hour ahead of standard time.

REFERENCE SECTION

Have you got the time?

What time is it?	Wie spät ist es?	vee shpait ist ehss
It's...	Es ist...	ehss ist
Excuse me. Can you tell me the time?	Verzeihung. Können Sie mir bitte sagen, wie spät es ist?	fehrtsighung. kurnern zee meer bitter zargern vee shpait ehss ist
I'll meet you at... tomorrow.	Ich treffe Sie morgen um...	ikh trehfer zee morgern um
I'm sorry I'm late.	Es tut mir leid, ich habe mich verspätet.	ehss toot meer light ikh harber mikh fehrshpaitert
At what time does... open?	Um wieviel Uhr öffnet...?	um veefeel oor urfnert
At what time does... close?	Um wieviel Uhr schließt...?	um veefeel oor shleest
How long will it last?	Wie lange wird es dauern?	vee langer veert ehss dowerrn
What time will it end?	Wann ist es zu Ende?	vahn ist ehss tsu ehnder
At what time should I be there?	Wann soll ich dort sein?	vahn zol ikh dort zighn
Can I come...?	Kann ich...kommen?	kahn ikh ... kommern
at 8 o'clock/at 2:30	um 8/um halb 3	um 8/um hahlp 3
after (prep.)	nach	narkh
afterwards	nachher	narkhhayr
before (prep.)	vor	foar
before	vorher	foarhayr
early	früh	frew
in time	rechtzeitig	rehkhttsightikh
late	spät	shpait
midnight	Mitternacht	mitterrnahkht
noon	Mittag	mittarg
hour	Stunde	shtunder
minute	Minute	minnooter
second	Sekunde	sehkunder
quarter of an hour	Viertelstunde	feerterlshtunder
half an hour	halbe Stunde	hahlber shtunder

Days

What day is it today?	Welchen Tag haben wir heute?	vehlkhern targ harbern veer hoyter
Sunday	Sonntag	zontarg
Monday	Montag	moantarg
Tuesday	Dienstag	deenstarg
Wednesday	Mittwoch	mitvokh
Thursday	Donnerstag	donnerrstarg
Friday	Freitag	frightarg
Saturday	Samstag/Sonnabend	zahmstarg/zonnarbernt
in the morning	am Morgen	ahm morgern
during the day	tagsüber	targsewberr
in the afternoon	am Nachmittag	ahm nahkhmittarg
in the evening	am Abend	ahm arbernt
at night	nachts	nahkhts
the day before yesterday	vorgestern	foargehsterrn
yesterday	gestern	gehsterrn
today	heute	hoyter
tomorrow	morgen	morgern
the day after tomorrow	übermorgen	ewberrmorgern
the day before	der vorhergehende Tag	derr foarhayrgayrnder targ
the next day	der Tag danach	derr targ dahnarkh
two days ago	vor zwei Tagen	foar tsvigh targern
in three days' time	in drei Tagen	in drigh targern
last week	letzte Woche	lehtster vokher
next week	nächste Woche	nehkhster vokher
for two weeks	zwei Wochen lang	tsvigh vokhern lahng
birthday	der Geburtstag	derr gerboortstarg
day	der Tag	derr targ
day off	der freie Tag	derr frigher targ
holiday	der Feiertag	derr figherrtarg
holidays	die Ferien	dee fayriern
month	der Monat	derr moanart
school holidays	die Schulferien	dee shoolfayriern
vacation	der Urlaub	derr oorlowp
week	die Woche	dee vokher
weekday	der Wochentag	derr vokherntarg
weekend	das Wochenende	dahss vokhernehnder
working day	der Werktag	derr vehrktarg

Months

January	**Januar**	yahnuarr
February	**Februar**	faybruarr
March	**März**	mehrts
April	**April**	ahpril
May	**Mai**	migh
June	**Juni**	yooni
July	**Juli**	yooli
August	**August**	owgust
September	**September**	sehptehmberr
October	**Oktober**	oktoaberr
November	**November**	noavehmberr
December	**Dezember**	daytsehmberr

since June	**seit Juni**	zight yooni
during the month of August	**während des Monats August**	vairernt dehss moanarts owgust
last month	**im letzten Monat**	im lehtstern moanart
next month	**im nächsten Monat**	im nehkhstern moanart
the month before	**der vorhergehende Monat**	derr foarhayrgayernder moanart
the month after	**der folgende Monat**	derr folgernder moanart
July 1	**der 1. Juli**	derr ehrster yooli
March 17	**der 17. März**	derr zeeptsaynter mehrts

Letter headings are written thus:

Munich, August 17, 19. . **München, den 17. August 19..**

Dusseldorf, July 1, 19. . **Düsseldorf, den 1. Juli 19..**

Seasons

spring	**der Frühling**	derr frewling
summer	**der Sommer**	derr sommerr
autumn	**der Herbst**	derr hehrpst
winter	**der Winter**	derr vinterr

in spring	**im Frühling**	im frewling
during the summer	**während des Sommers**	vairernt dehss sommerrs
in autumn	**im Herbst**	im hehrpst
during the winter	**während des Winters**	vairernt dehss vinterrs

Public holidays

Only national holidays in Germany (D), Austria (A) or Switzerland (CH) are cited below.

Jan. 1	**Neujahr**	New Year's Day	D A CH
Jan. 2			CH*
Jan. 6	**Heilige 3 Könige**	Epiphany	A
May 1	**Tag der Arbeit**	Labour Day	D A
June 17	**Tag der Deutschen Einheit**	National Unity Day	D
Aug. 1	**Nationalfeiertag**	National Day	CH*
Aug. 15	**Mariä Himmelfahrt**	Assumption Day	A
Oct. 26	**Nationalfeiertag**	National Day	A
Nov. 1	**Allerheiligen**	All Saints' Day	A
Dec. 8	**Unbefleckte Empfängnis**	Immaculate Conception	A
Dec. 25	**1. Weihnachtstag**	Christmas Day	D A CH
Dec. 26	**2. Weihnachtstag**	St. Stephen's Day	D A CH*
Movable dates:	**Karfreitag**	Good Friday	D CH*
	Ostermontag	Easter Monday	D A CH
	Christi Himmelfahrt	Ascension	D A CH
	Pfingstmontag	Whit Monday	D A CH
	Fronleichnam	Corpus Christi	A

* Most cantons

The year round...

	Hamburg	Munich	Vienna	Zurich
January	35.6°F	33.8°F	33.8°F	35.6°F
February	37.4	37.4	37.4	41.0
March	46.4	48.2	46.4	50.0
April	55.4	57.2	57.2	59.0
May	64.4	64.4	66.2	66.2
June	71.6	69.8	71.6	73.4
July	73.4	73.4	77.0	77.0
August	73.4	73.4	75.2	75.2
September	66.2	68.0	68.0	68.0
October	55.4	55.4	57.2	57.2
November	44.6	44.6	44.6	44.6
December	39.2	35.6	37.4	37.4

Common abbreviations

ACS	Automobil-Club der Schweiz	Automobile Association of Switzerland
ADAC	Allgemeiner Deutscher Automobil-Club	General Automobile Association of Germany
a. M.	am Main	on the Main River
a. Rh.	am Rhein	on the Rhine River
AvD	Automobil-Club von Deutschland	Automobile Club of Germany
Bhf	Bahnhof	railway station
BRD	Bundesrepublik Deutschland	Federal Republic of Germany (West Germany)
DB	Deutsche Bundesbahn	Federal German Railway
DDR	Deutsche Demokratische Republik	German Democratic Republic (East Germany)
d. h.	das heißt	i.e. (that is)
DIN	Deutsche Industrie-Norm	German Industrial Standard
Frl.	Fräulein	Miss
G.	Gasse	lane
Hbf.	Hauptbahnhof	main railway station
Hr.	Herr	Mr.
LKW	Lastkraftwagen	lorry/truck
MEZ	Mitteleuropäische Zeit	Central European Time
Mio.	Million	million
Mrd.	Milliarde	1000 millions (billion)
n. Chr.	nach Christus	A.D.
ÖAMTC	Österreichischer Automobil-Motorrad- und Touring-Club	Austrian Automobile, Motorcycle and Touring Association
ÖBB	Österreichische Bundesbahnen	Austrian Federal Railways
PKW	Personenkraftwagen	motor car
Pl.	Platz	square
PS	Pferdestärke	horsepower
PTT	Post, Telephon, Telegraph	Post, Telephone and Telegraph Office
SBB	Schweizerische Bundesbahnen	Swiss Federal Railways
St.	Stock	floor
Str.	Straße	street
TCS	Touring-Club der Schweiz	Swiss Touring Club
usw.	und so weiter	etc.
v. Chr.	vor Christus	B.C.
z. B.	zum Beispiel	e.g. (for example)
z. Z.	zur Zeit	at present

Conversion tables

Centimetres and inches

To change centimetres into inches, multiply by .39.

To change inches into centimetres, multiply by 2.54.

	in.	feet	yards
1 mm	0,039	0,003	0,001
1 cm	0,39	0,03	0,01
1 dm	3,94	0,32	0,10
1 m	39,40	3,28	1,09

	mm	cm	m
1 in.	25,4	2,54	0,025
1 ft.	304,8	30,48	0,304
1 yd.	914,4	91,44	0,914

(32 metres = 35 yards)

Temperature

To convert Centigrade into degrees Fahrenheit, multiply Centigrade by 1.8 and add 32.

To convert degrees Fahrenheit into Centigrade, subtract 32 from Fahrenheit and divide by 1.8.

Metres and feet

The figure in the middle stands for both metres and feet, e.g.,
1 metre = 3.281 ft. and 1 foot = 0.30 m.

Metres		Feet
0.30	1	3.281
0.61	2	6.563
0.91	3	9.843
1.22	4	13.124
1.52	5	16.403
1.83	6	19.686
2.13	7	22.967
2.44	8	26.248
2.74	9	29.529
3.05	10	32.810
3.35	11	36.091
3.66	12	39.372
3.96	13	42.635
4.27	14	45.934
4.57	15	49.215
4.88	16	52.496
5.18	17	55.777
5.49	18	59.058
5.79	19	62.339
6.10	20	65.620
7.62	25	82.023
15.24	50	164.046
22.86	75	246.069
30.48	100	328.092

Other conversion charts

Weight conversion

The figure in the middle stands for both kilograms and pounds, e.g., 1 kilogram = 2.205 1b. and 1 pound = 0.45 kilograms.

Kilograms (kg.)		Avoirdupois pounds
0.45	1	2.205
0.90	2	4.405
1.35	3	6.614
1.80	4	8.818
2.25	5	11.023
2.70	6	13.227
3.15	7	15.432
3.60	8	17.636
4.05	9	19.840
4.50	10	22.045
6.75	15	33.068
9.00	20	44.889
11.25	25	55.113
22.50	50	110.225
33.75	75	165.338
45.00	100	220.450

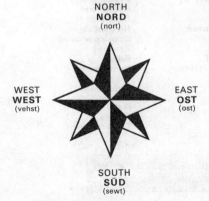

NORTH
NORD
(nort)

WEST
WEST
(vehst)

EAST
OST
(ost)

SOUTH
SÜD
(sewt)

REFERENCE SECTION

What does that sign mean?

Achtung	Caution
Aufzug	Lift (elevator)
Ausgang	Exit
Auskunft	Information
Ausverkauf	Sales
Ausverkauft	Sold out
Besetzt	Occupied
Bitte klingeln	Please ring
Drücken	Push
Eingang	Entrance
Eintreten ohne zu klopfen	Enter without knocking
Eintritt frei	No admission charge
Frei	Vacant
Für Unbefugte verboten	No trepassing
Gefahr	Danger
Geschlossen	Closed
Heiß	Hot
Kalt	Cold
Kasse	Cashier's
Kein Zutritt	No entrance
Lebensgefahr	Danger of death
Lift	Lift (elevator)
Nicht berühren	Do not touch
Nichtraucher	No smoking
Notausgang	Emergency exit
Nur für Anlieger	Residents only
Privatweg	Private road
Radweg	Cycle path
Rauchen verboten	No smoking
Raucher	Smoking allowed
Reserviert	Reserved
Schlußverkauf	Sales
Unbefugtes Betreten verboten	No trepassing
...verboten	...forbidden
Vorsicht	Caution
Ziehen	Pull
Zu verkaufen	For sale
Zu vermieten	To let (for hire)

VORSICHT, BISSIGER HUND
BEWARE OF THE DOG

Emergency

By the time the emergency is upon you it's too late to turn to this page to find the German for "I'll scream if you...". So have a look at this short list beforehand—and, if you want to be on the safe side, learn the expressions shown in capitals.

Be quick	**Schnell**	shnehl
Call the police	**Rufen Sie die Polizei**	roofern zee dee poalitsigh
CAREFUL	**VORSICHT**	foarzikht
Come here	**Kommen Sie her**	kommern zee hayr
FIRE	**FEUER**	foyerr
Gas	**Gas**	gahss
Get a doctor	**Holen Sie einen Arzt**	hoalern zee ighnern ahrtst
Go away	**Gehen Sie weg**	gayern zee vehk
HELP	**HILFE**	hilfer
Get help quickly	**Holen Sie schnell Hilfe**	hoalern zee shnehl hilfer
I'm ill	**Ich bin krank**	ikh bin krahnk
I'm lost	**Ich habe mich verrirt**	ikh harber mikh fehreert
I've lost...	**Ich habe...verloren**	ikh harber ... fehrloarern
Keep your hands to yourself	**Hände weg**	hehnder vehk
Leave me alone	**Lassen Sie mich in Ruhe**	lahssern zee mikh in rooer
Look out	**Passen Sie auf**	pahssern zee owf
POLICE	**POLIZEI**	politsigh
Quick	**Schnell**	shnehl
STOP	**HALT**	hahlt
Stop that man	**Haltet den Mann**	hahltert dayn mahn
STOP THIEF	**HALTET DEN DIEB**	hahltert dayn deep
Stop or I'll scream	**Halt oder ich schreie**	hahlt oaderr ikh shrigher

Emergency telephone numbers

	Austria	Germany	Switzerland
Fire	122	112	118
Police	133	110	117

FOR CAR ACCIDENTS, see page 150

REFERENCE SECTION

Index

Quick reference page

Here are some phrases and expressions which you'll probably need most frequently on your trip:

Please.	**Bitte.**	bitter
Thank you.	**Danke schön.**	dahngker shurn
Yes/No.	**Ja/Nein.**	yar/nighn
Excuse me.	**Verzeihung!**	fehrtsighung
Waiter, please!	**Herr Ober!**	hehr oaberr
How much is that?	**Wieviel macht es?**	veefeel mahkht ehss
Where are the toilets?	**Wo sind die Toiletten?**	voa zint dee toaahlehtern

WC/00/Toiletten	Toilets
Herren (hehrern)	**Damen** (darmern)

REFERENCE SECTION

Can you tell me...?	**Können Sie mir sagen...?**	kurnern zee meer zargern
where/when/why	**wo/wann/warum**	voa/vahn/vahrum
Help me, please.	**Helfen Sie mir, bitte.**	hehlfern zee meer bitter
Where is the... consulate?	**Wo ist das... Konsulat?**	voa ist dahss... konzoolaht
American	**amerikanische**	ahmehreekarneescher
British	**britische**	britisher
Canadian	**kanadische**	kahnahdeesher
What does this mean? I don't understand.	**Was bedeutet das? Ich verstehe nicht.**	vahss berdoytert dahss? ikh fehrshtayer nikht
Do you speak English?	**Sprechen Sie Englisch?**	shprehkhern zee ehnglish